To and Fro
the Ivory Tower

Life in Academia

Pamela J. Farris
Northern Illinois University

and

Marilyn K. Moore
Illinois State University

WAVELAND

PRESS, INC.

Long Grove, Illinois

For information about this book, contact:
Waveland Press, Inc.
4180 IL Route 83, Suite 101
Long Grove, IL 60047-9580
(847) 634-0081
info@waveland.com
www.waveland.com

Disclaimer: Each institution has its own rules and regulations regarding employment, tenure, promotion, and retirement. This book offers some career suggestions that are generally appropriate at most universities in the United States. An individual, must, of course, familiarize himself/herself with the culture and regulations of his/her department, college, and university.

Photo credits

Cover: Kay Moss Photography: http://www.kaymossphotography.com/

Interior: 5 Mccartm8,Wikimedia Commons/Creative Commons Attribution-Share Alike 3.0 license; **19** Robert J. LaVerghetta, Wikimedia Commons/GNU Free Documentation License, Version 1.2 or any later version published by the Free Software Foundation; **41** Bhockey10, Wikimedia Commons/Creative Commons Attribution-Share Alike 3.0 license; **44** Bluejayscholar, Wikimedia Commons/Creative Commons Attribution-Share Alike 3.0 license; **55** Nyttend, Wikimedia Commons/Public Domain; **61** Bhockey10, Wikimedia Commons/GNU Free Documentation License, Version 1.2 or any later version published by the Free Software Foundation; **79** M.Fitzsimmons, Wikimedia Commons/Creative Commons Attribution-Share Alike 3.0 license; **87** Another Believer, Wikimedia Commons/ Creative Commons Attribution-Share Alike 3.0 license; **93** User:Akendall, Wikimedia Commons/GNU Free Documentation License, Version 1.2 or any later version published by the Free Software Foundation; **98** James Steakley, Wikimedia Commons/Creative Commons Attribution-Share Alike 3.0 license; **103** Tony Strong/Shutterstock.com; **108** Leoboudv, Wikimedia Commons/Creative Commons Attribution-Share Alike 3.0 license

Printed in the United States of America

7 6 5 4 3 2 1

Contents

Foreword

Who among us would not welcome a road map to guide us through choosing an academic career, the steps we will take in order to progress, and then, finally, to say good-bye to almost everything that has created our professional identity? Pamela Farris and Marilyn Moore have provided us with such a road map, a guide to the various points on the road where we must make a decision that could affect every part of our future life.

To and Fro the Ivory Tower takes us first to the decision to embark on a doctoral degree, what considerations must be made, and what choices must be examined. The black-and-white movie version of a college professor who exists in an ivory tower does not hold true today. The world of university teaching instead includes online instruction, teaching at branch campuses, developing curriculum for MOOCs, global diversity, and responding to emails at 5:00 in the morning.

While some universities provide extensive professional development, mentoring, and grooming to junior faculty, many simply don't have the time or resources to spend on such activities. As growing numbers of the "boomer" generation prepare for retirement, we face a losing race to replace the tenure-track faculty who are leaving the ranks of professor. *To and Fro the Ivory Tower* provides practical considerations for those who are anticipating a doctorate, considering a teaching position at a college or university, and then moving up the ladder of promotion and tenure. Significant attention is paid to "helpful hints" that usually are not shared by those already in the tenure track with newly hired faculty. From "Read your contract carefully" to "Don't let this happen to you," Farris and Moore's valuable advice covers a variety of academic levels and time frames: the beginning tenure-track position, the associate and full professor positions, and even what to expect in retirement. They provide helpful advice for those returning to faculty status from administration or those who are switching gears from a regional campus to a larger or research institutions.

Written from the perspective of longtime teachers, professors, Chairs, and authors of multiple books on teaching and learning, *To and Fro the Ivory Tower* funnels years of practical experience into a road map for college and university faculty.

Susan M. Cooper, Ed.D.
Dean, Irvine Campus
California State University, Fullerton

Prologue

Why Do I Want to Be a Professor Anyway?

Most people who have chosen to become a professor know it takes dedication and hard work. The Chair of your dissertation has placed a sash over your head and straightened it out over your shoulders. Now that you are "hooded," people will refer to you as "doctor"; there is no better academic feeling than to hear your name announced with the abbreviation Dr. placed before it.

When making your choice to become a college professor, you probably considered the following questions:

1. Will my area of study result in a job where my earnings compensate any debt I have as well as future living expenses?
2. Am I looking at my career over the long term, with regard to all the factors involved, including where I will be living and retirement benefits?
3. Am I interested in working with both undergraduate and graduate students?
4. Are there other career opportunities, in addition to those in a university or college setting, in which having doctorate degree is required or useful?

Today, many university departments of Education, Engineering, the Biological Sciences, and Nursing currently have faculty openings for which PhDs in those fields can apply. There are also jobs in the private sector for those with doctorates as well. An abundance of openings enables these new doctorate job-seekers to select the location in which they prefer to live. However, the likelihood of a new doctorate in English, History, Philosophy, or Fine Arts landing a faculty position at a university, liberal arts college, or community college is extremely slim, as these areas have far more applicants than openings—sometimes over a 100 applicants for a single assistant professor position. The table below (U.S. Census, 2012) lists the doctorates awarded by field of study and year of doctorate.

Doctorates Awarded by Field of Study and Year of Doctorate: 2000 to 2009

[Based on the *Survey of Earned Doctorates*; for information, see source]

Field of Study	2000	2004	2005	2006	2007	2008	2009
Total, all fields	41,366	42,118	43,381	45,617	48,130	48,763	49,562
Science and engineering, total	25,966	26,274	27,986	29,866	31,806	32,832	33,470
Engineering, total	5,323	5,777	6,427	7,185	7,745	7,859	7,634
Aeronautical/ astronomical	214	201	219	238	267	266	296
Chemical	619	638	774	799	807	872	808
Civil	480	547	622	655	701	712	708
Electrical	1,330	1,389	1,547	1,786	1,968	1,887	1,694
Industrial/ manufacturing	176	217	221	234	281	280	252
Materials/ metallurgical	404	474	493	583	648	635	622
Mechanical	807	754	892	1,044	1,072	1,081	1,095
Other	1,293	1,557	1,659	1,846	2,001	2,126	2,159
Science, total	20,643	20,497	21,559	22,681	24,061	24,973	25,836
Biological/agricultural sciences	6,890	6,987	7,404	7,682	8,320	8,885	9192
Agricultural sciences	1,037	1,045	1,038	1,033	1,133	1,087	1,166
Biological sciences	5,853	5,942	6,366	6,649	7,187	7,798	8,026

(continued)

Earth, atmospheric, and ocean sciences, total	694	686	714	757	878	865	877
Atmospheric	143	126	145	146	167	188	167
Earth/ocean sciences	551	560	569	611	711	677	710
Mathematical/ computer sciences, total	1,911	2,024	2,334	2,778	3,049	3,186	3,165
Computer sciences	861	948	1,129	1,453	1,656	1,787	1,611
Mathematics	1,050	1,076	1,205	1,325	1,393	1,399	1,554
Physical sciences, total	3,378	3,335	3,643	3,927	4,101	4,082	4,289
Astronomy	185	165	186	197	223	249	262
Chemistry	1,989	1,986	2,126	2,362	2,324	2,247	2,398
Physics	1,204	1,184	1,331	1,368	1,554	1,586	1,629
Psychology	3,615	3,326	3,323	3,260	3,291	3,356	3,471
Social sciences, total	4,155	4,139	4,141	4,277	4,422	4,599	4,842
Economics	1,086	1,069	1,183	1,142	1,180	1,202	1,237
Political science	986	947	990	1,001	1,037	1,020	1,140
Sociology	617	580	536	579	576	601	664
Other social sciences	1,466	1,543	1,432	1,555	1,629	1,776	1,801
Non-science and engineering, total	**15,400**	**15,844**	**15,395**	**15,751**	**16,324**	**15,931**	**16,092**
Education	6,437	6,633	6,225	6,120	6,456	6,554	6,531
Health	1,591	1,719	1,784	1,905	2,132	2,090	2,094
Humanities	5,213	5,012	4,950	5,124	4,890	4,502	4,667
Professional/other/ unknown	2,159	2,480	2,436	2,602	2,846	2,785	2,800

Source: U.S. National Science Foundation, *Science and Engineering Doctorate Awards*, annual. See also http://www.nsf.gov/statistics/doctorates/

When you decided entering academic life is for you, you may have visited a university/college and met with a professor or two in your area of study, armed with well-prepared questions to discover what it is like to be a professor at that university/college. This meeting should have given you a much broader picture of the university's, as well as the department's, expectations—from academic preparation and focus to teaching, service, and scholarship in the field. You most likely came away with and weighed both the positive and the negative aspects of academic life at that institution.

It is not unusual to go home and to still feel nervous about embarking on a big challenge. Likely, though, something in you will make you say, "I really want to give this a good try and I know I will feel badly if I don't." If you still feel nervous, however, and there is not that call within you to move forward with the challenge, it is probably better to give yourself more time to think it through.

Hopefully, you checked out a variety of opportunities and found that the quality of the institution is not the only important factor to consider—that other factors affected your decision to take a job. Perhaps your main goal was to work with noted researchers in the field. Or, you were interested in being mentored by the Chair of the Department, choosing a school whose Department Chair is known for nurturing new faculty in both teaching and research. Knowing in advance which administrative duties are required might have been high on your list of priorities, as well as the required teaching load. Most top-notch universities expect faculty to conduct research and publish the results in academic journals and present papers at conferences; if you are more interested in teaching than in conducting research, you may have steered clear of institutions that emphasize publishing and presenting. However, in order to gain tenure and promotion, you will have to publish in refereed journals in your field and present papers at conferences in your discipline regardless of the college or university that hires you. Failure to do so will result in your dismissal.

Opposite page: Anderson Hall, Miami University, Oxford, Ohio.

1

The Search

If you are reading this book prior to being hired at an academic institution, you'll find the guidelines that take you through the job-search, application, interview, and hiring processes presented in this chapter to be a tremendous help. Arming yourself with this chapter's information means you don't have to start from scratch—you'll know what to expect and what is expected of you. If you have already accepted a job, you may still want to review this chapter in the event you find your institution is not a good fit for you and you decide to search for a job at another institution.

The Candidate's Perspective

Every day or week you search the *Chronicle of Higher Education* website and your professional organization's listserves for new position postings. Listings increase as the academic year moves deep into autumn, then comes a new surge of listings just after New Year's Day as institutions finalize their needs based on pending retirements by current faculty as well as program expansion due to demand, and budgets begin to gel. You bookmark or print out those that look most appealing—the Southeast Conference school with the dream research lab, the university in the Rockies that pays in scenery (but that's fine with you), the California university with a perfect job description to match to your background and close proximity to the beach, urban universities surrounded by sky-scrapers, the Big Ten university that you've always wanted to be a part of, and the small, well-endowed private college that tugs at your heartstrings because it's reminiscent of the alma mater of your undergraduate years.

You've resolved to find the ideal faculty position where you'll teach, conduct notable research, and write an endless number of peer reviewed articles and books to bring fame, if not fortune, to yourself and your institution. During your doctoral program, you've created a respect-able curriculum vitae (CV) with a number of refereed publications and papers read at national and regional conferences held by professional organizations in your field of study. Academia, here you come!

Do Your Homework

Where to begin? How does one focus? On the research demands of certain colleges? On a region of the country that is desirable to you? On a location that is new and different for you? Do you want to move to be close to family or friends? Do you send out as many applications as there are jobs, or do you selectively choose the institutions? If there is a shortage of applicants in your field, you can be more selective in where you apply. During tight economic times, some job positions will be eliminated by universities as they attempt to manage their budgets by covering positions for another year with a temporary faculty member before actually hiring a tenure-track person for the opening.

Do you really want to teach in a state or region where you can't stand the heat/humidity/cold/snow/politics? Or are you willing to take a position for a short time, such as one or two years, establish a scholarly record, and get a grant or two before moving on to a more desirable institution? Should you do a post-doc, taking a research position in order to gain employment at another research university?

What about salary? Each April, the American Association of University Professors (AAUP) posts a survey of salaries of faculty by rank (assistant, associate, professor) by state in the *Chronicle of Higher Education*. While the salaries are averaged across departments and colleges, the results are indicative of salary ranges at different institutions. Also a Google search of the pension system of a state institution is a wise move, given that many states might be cutting pension benefits of the public universities and community colleges.

Accessing the university's website can provide more information. Googling the city in which the college is located and considering the demographics of the community at large (median income, representation of diversity in the population, housing costs, level of education for residents, crime rate, and so on) provides additional data to aid in making an informed decision. Do you want to live in a locale where you can walk to campus and take public transportation to shopping and entertainment? Or in a city with public parks and bike trails?

Should you ask your Doctoral Committee members about different institutions? They likely have developed networks in the field that can readily open doors or provide valuable information. For instance, a doctoral student was planning to apply to a major university in the east and her Dissertation Chair pointed out that that particular institution was noted for hiring two or three assistant professors at one time and then, after a couple of years, dismissing the individual who had the weakest teaching reviews and lowest number of scholarly publications, papers presented, and grant submissions. Your fellow doctoral students, too, are seeking employment in your field, and they can be helpful in sharing information they may have gathered. But be aware that they may desire the same position that interests you. One doctoral student was aghast that someone she considered a good friend out maneuvered her in getting a position at a university across the city. The doctoral student had discovered the opening and talked it up to her friend who quietly made contacts with that institution's faculty a few weeks later at a professional conference at which she presented a paper. She even managed to join a few of them for dinner at the conference. Both doctoral students were interviewed, but the position was offered to the friend, not to the one who had "discovered" the opening.

Application Packet

Your application packet should include the letter of application, your curriculum vitae (CV) (your degrees, employment history, scholarly publications, grant proposals, and presentations at professional meetings), a copy of your transcript (generally a photocopy is sufficient for the interview, with an official copy supplied if you accept the position), and list of professional references. Some departments request a writing sample of an article or book chapter of which you are sole author. Other departments may ask you to write a philosophical statement, research statement, or address a current issue in your field. Copies of course syllabi and course evaluations by students may also be requested.

These materials are all uploaded as part of the college or university's human resources website for job applications. Letters from your references should be sent directly by those individuals writing your recommendations to the institution as a blind review without your handling them.

Keep in mind some institutions don't require a letter unless you are selected for the interview, so you need to note the differences as you apply.

If letters of recommendation are required, be sure to make your requests in ample time so those writing the letters aren't rushed. Two weeks before the due date is appropriate. Also, you can check with the university to which you are applying to see if the letters arrived or were attached appropriately. And don't forget to send a handwritten thank-you note to each person who wrote a letter of recommendation.

Submit your application at least five business days prior to the deadline date for submissions. This gives you time in case there is a computer glitch. Also it gives you a buffer as sometimes the first applicants are overly scrutinized by members of the committee. Make certain to proofread everything before sending the application packet. Also, putting all of your materials in a small, thin binder that you bring with you should you be invited for an on-campus interview delivers a professional image of your work to the Search Committee.

Some institutions stipulate in the posting that the review of applications will begin at a specific date and will continue until the position is filled. This is a moving target, in effect, but it is always best to get your application in a few days before the review is to begin. Some institutions will email you once your file is complete. However, others will not. It is up to you to inquire as to whether all your materials have successfully been uploaded at the institution.

The Letter of Application

The letter of application is your introduction to the Search Committee and the Department Chair. It must address your strengths and weaknesses (preferably far more positives than negatives) as they relate to the job. While it may seem more efficient to crank identical application letters, thoughtfully crafting a well-worded letter of application tailored specifically to the position requirements will bring attention to your candidacy and increase the likelihood of an invitation to campus.

Begin the letter on a positive note, then move to your own skills as they relate to the position requirements. You may want to use bullet points to point out specifically how your skillset dovetails with the needs of the position. It is important to be positive but avoid being too casual. The next paragraph should provide an overview of your work and research experience or quality papers presented at major conferences. Any refereed publications should be noted. Conclude with your desire to be at that institution. Have someone proof your letter for grammatical errors and typos. If possible, a person from a university would be a good proof reader/advisor because he/she will have a sense of what universities look for and what they find inappropriate or weak. In short, market yourself so that the readers of the letter believe you are a good fit for the position. You may use up to two full pages and, if you are permitted, use your university department's letterhead. Avoid overpraising yourself. One candidate once wrote, "I believe I would be an incredible person for you to hire. People I work with now actually say, "I am stupendous." And yet another wrote his own letter of recommendation in the third person and signed it.

Be sure you put your cell phone number and your email address on your application letter and your CV as these will be the contact information used at the department level. Also include your professional address or home address where the check for your travel for an interview and hopefully the offering letter for the position is to be sent.

Curriculum Vitae

Your curriculum vitae (CV) is the shortened version of your professional life. In the business world it is called a resume. The CV should include your name, current address, email address (personal rather than one for institution you are attending), and cell phone number centered at the top of the page, followed by your education history, with the doctorate listed first, then your master's and bachelor's degrees listed next to the institutions that awarded the degrees. You may choose to list the years you graduated but are not bound to do so. Any honors (summa cum laude, etc.) should be listed where appropriate. If you are ABD (all but dissertation), and have an established defense date, include it. Also list the title of your dissertation, and you may include, in parentheses, your Dissertation Chair.

Next, list your experience in the field, again with you most recent job first. This is followed by your research, which may be only your dissertation title, grants, publications, papers presented at conferences, and memberships in professional organizations. Any joint publications

Sample Letter of Application
(on Letterhead of Doctoral Department)

January 17, 2014
Dr. Jerome MacNeill, Chair
Department of Biological Sciences
University of Missouri
Columbia, MO 65311

Dear Dr. MacNeill:

Please accept this letter of application for the position of Assistant Professor of Biology/Cell Biology. In reading the position statement, I believe my past experiences offer a good fit for this position.

The title of my dissertation is "Stem Cell Niches: The Use of Stem Cells with Parkinson's Patients" with the defense scheduled for April 15, 2014. My dissertation director is Dr. Spencer Sudcliff, a pioneer in the use of stem cells. My research demonstrates promise in reducing the tremors of later stage Parkinson's.

During my doctoral pursuit I have co-presented three refereed papers at major conferences with Dr. Sudcliff. In addition, I have presented a paper at a regional conference. Currently I have one refereed coauthored article published in the *Journal of Stem Cell Research* and another manuscript presently under review with *The Parkinson's Research Journal.*

At the University of Georgia, I have taught the introductory course in Cell Biology as well as the initial course in Cell and Molecular Biology. My student ratings (attached) have been favorable and I was nominated for the college instructor award for teaching by a TA.

Thank you and the Search Committee for your consideration of this application for the position.

Sincerely,
Jennifer Jensen, Teaching Assistant
Department of Chemistry
University of Georgia
Athens, GA 30602
789-456-1235
jjensen@comcast.net

or presentations should be listed along with the order of importance of each individual's contributions (i.e., if you are the secondary author, list your name as such or as it appeared in the journal or on the paper). You need to think about building a strong, well-balanced CV while you are still taking coursework and beginning your dissertation. Offer to engage in research with a faculty member and then co-present at a conference. If that work is published you've thereby yielded two lines on your CV. Submit for a grant, even if it is for a very small amount. Colleges and universities are looking for faculty who can bring in external funding, and even a $1,000 grant proposal will set you apart from someone who has never applied for one. Enhancing your CV takes many months or even years before you put it together in the application process.

When listing your publications, use the appropriate reference format, MLA or APA according to your field of study. Don't pad your CV, as phantom listings could come back to haunt you when you go up for tenure/promotion, if not sooner. Search Committees will go to the library and look up articles, for instance, so make certain everything listed is accurate and up to date. If you interview during the spring semester, and had a presentation or published an article after you submitted your application, update your CV and bring to the interview as well as sending the updated version to the Department Chair. Always date your CV at the bottom of the last page and as part of your computer file name (i.e., JohnsonvitaOct2014).

References

Selecting individuals to serve as references is a major decision. Generally speaking, have members of both sexes on your list of references. Besides your major professor, you may want to include another professor plus an administrator who is familiar with your work. Administrators tend to have connections with administrators at other institutions, a plus if the Department Chair or the Dean has the final hiring decision. Certainly well-known professors' names can get the attention of Search Committee members, but sometimes well-known professors are too busy to return phone calls for references or even write a letter of recommendation. Worse, the distinguished professor writes a generic recommendation letter for all newly minted PhDs.

Sample Curriculum Vitae

Jason T. Slocum
1234 Pacific Lane
Los Angeles, CA 95432
920-753-1234

Education:
PhD History—University of Southern California (defense April 4, 2014)
MA History—University of Colorado
BA History—University of Missouri

Employment:
2012–2014   Teaching Assistant—University of Southern California
2011–2012   Graduate Assistant—University of Colorado

Dissertation:
"A Comparison of Two American Generals: General John Pershing and General George Patton." Chaired by Professor Thomas Mason.

Publications:
Slocum, J. T. and T. Mason. "Strategies used by World War I generals as compared to World War II in Europe." In J. Smith (Ed.), *The World Wars: A Comparison,* pp. 56–78. New York: Maxwell Publishing, 2014.

Papers Presented:
Slocum, J. T. "Pershing and Patton: A Comparison of Two Army Generals." American History Association, New Orleans, LA, March 2, 2014.

Memberships:
American History Association

Service:
Board Member, Graduate Student Association, University of Southern California
Treasurer, Student Historical Society

The process of deciding who to ask to be your references should start long before you make the request. You can't just hope they will think you are well suited for a university position. You have to prove this to them over time. They have to see consistency in your work ethic, your scholarly abilities, and your positive interaction with colleagues. If you teach undergraduates, you need to have favorable ratings that indicate students respect you as an instructor.

Verification of Receipt

After your mailed application package should have been received or has been submitted online, you may wish to verify that the institution received your materials. An email to the person listed in the college ad requesting confirmation is appropriate. Most online applications let you see that the attachments have been successfully or unsuccessfully uploaded. You may receive a letter from the department via email or snail mail, usually along with a brief survey from the college's affirmative action office regarding the position. Sometimes this information is requested online as part of the application process. This survey represents general data collection, so the institution can verify to the federal government that it is an equal opportunity employer (EOE) and does not discriminate against applicants based on race/color or gender.

The Screening Process

Most universities have the Search Committee screen and narrow the pool of applicants to a "long list" of perhaps four to six candidates. The Search Committee has a rubric against which all applicants' qualifications are evaluated. If the job description specifies that the applicant must possess a doctorate, ABDs (All But Dissertation) won't be considered. Or someone from the department may call to find out if a dissertation defense date has been established. Thus, the sooner in the academic year you can defend, the better it looks on your application.

An instructor or teaching assistant from the institution offering the faculty position may apply, and if that individual obtained a doctorate from another institution, the likelihood of getting an interview is far greater than if the individual obtained his/her doctorate from the institution offering the faculty position. If that individual has a record of being a good instructor, has a number of publications, and made several presentations, that individual will have an inside track on the position.

The job description or ad will include two types of qualifications: (1) required and (2) preferred. Any requirements that are specified in the job description *must* be completely met by the applicant. You can't meet two of the four or three of the four. You must meet all four requirements if four are listed. An applicant doesn't need to possess all the preferred qualifications that are usually listed beneath the requirements for the position. But any additional qualifications that meet those listed in the job description may give that applicant an advantage over the others in the pool. These may be grants, publications, and/or presentations, as well as work experience, particularly teaching at the university level. Preferred qualifications are generally extra skills or specialties that would enhance the offerings of the department for students.

During the screening process some applicants' CVs typically stand out over those of others. The individuals who have outstanding CVs will have presented papers at noteworthy conferences in the field and perhaps have a refereed publication in a national journal or at least one in press. Previous positions held by the applicants may demonstrate a solid background of experience. Outstanding CVs also contain references from faculty and colleagues who convey they know the applicants and their expertise.

The Search Committee's written justification for selecting particular applicants to be interviewed as part of the first round (phone interviews only) goes to the Department Chair who then suggests modifications in the wording or accepts the document before forwarding the information to the university's affirmative action office, which reviews the list of applicants to make certain all received a fair evaluation.

The Phone Interview

After the affirmative action officer has approved the list of candidates, the Search Committee moves to the next step, calling each candidate on the long list and conducting a conference call. The Search Committee establishes a protocol of set questions that are asked of each candidate during the phone call. These questions will vary based on the institution and the specifications for the position, including required and preferred qualifications. A specified time length for the phone call, usually about 30 to 45 minutes, is determined. Next, a secretary or member of the Search Committee contacts the candidates and sets up the time and date for the phone interviews.

For you, the candidate, phone interviews can be tricky for a number of reasons. For example, the committee does not have an opportunity to read your body language over the phone, which is why it is important that you are prepared, confident in your conversational skills, and well informed. While members of the Search Committee will introduce themselves, it is sometimes difficult for you to discern which name goes with which voice as the interview proceeds. If possible, write down the names of the members as they introduce themselves, as typically they will go around the table when they ask the questions.

The questions the Search Committee members will ask are fairly generic:

- Why are you interested in this position?
- What do you believe you will add to our program or department?
- Who are the major researchers/theorists who have influenced your own research?
- If you were to work at our institution, what would you imagine your typical week to be like?
- What is your philosophy regarding your field of study?
- Everyone has strengths and areas in which they need more development. What do you feel are yours?
- Do you have any questions for the committee?

Prepare yourself for the phone interview by doing thorough advance work. How you respond to the questions makes the difference between being invited for an on-campus visit or receiving a letter several weeks later saying, while you have several worthwhile qualities, the department selected another candidate to fill the position. Check out articles written by faculty from the department to get a feel for their interests and research. Go online and peruse the department's course offerings and programs of study, both undergraduate and graduate. To prepare for the phone interview, try to anticipate what will be asked and write your answers/notes for each question. This will not only help clarify your own position but make you appear as an organized thinker. Some candidates role-play the interview by having a friend call and ask questions interview questions.

Your answers should be clear and concise—rambling on and on is not in your best interest. If a questioner throws you a curve, it is acceptable to make a statement to buy a bit of time while you can create a response. However, don't keep saying "That's a difficult question" to stall until you can formulate your answer.

If you sense a divisive committee, you may either stay in a neutral position or lean toward what you believe to be the majority position. Make sure you have prepared at least one relevant question about the program of study and another about the community where the college is. Other pertinent questions can be about class size and research support (i.e., use of a lab, university funding for internal grants, travel expenses to conferences). It is appropriate to inquire about the course load and number of course preparations as well as graduate assistant assignments. Such questions show you have done some research (such as reading information on the department's website and having Googled the institution to see if there are major developments such as a new research lab or a huge grant award) about the prospective job.

Become familiar with the mission statement of the college and reference it during your phone (and, if one is scheduled, your in-person) interview. It is important to mention it up front so the Search Committee knows you are well informed before they ask you if you can address it. As mentioned earlier, closely examine the undergraduate and graduate courses offered by the institution. One candidate accepted a position at a university only to learn that the courses he was to teach were two (2) credit hours, which meant he had an extra prep each week. He resigned after the first year. Had he checked the college catalog for the courses in the department in which he was interviewing, he probably wouldn't have agreed to even the phone interview.

Avoid taboo topics. Don't inquire about salary—the Department Chair will address salary and benefits during the on-campus interview. Don't ask how much time faculty are expected to spend on campus or the minimum number of office hours faculty are expected to hold. These questions may be interpreted as a lack of work ethic rather than just a matter of interest. After the phone interview, don't email the Search Committee to belabor a point. For example, at the end of the phone interview, you learn that you won't always have a choice of specific courses you will teach, but your will teach courses in your field of experience. Even if this lack of choice doesn't appeal to you, don't email faculty on the committee saying that there are only certain courses you would consider teaching and you would like to know if that is acceptable if you were offered the position. Conducting yourself in this way presents a "red flag" to the Search Committee. You have to decide if the lack of course selection is acceptable or unacceptable, and if it's the latter, cross that institution off your list.

Do insert levity, if appropriate, as everyone will relax. But make it a neutral topic such as weather or travel. Make certain to be pleasant throughout the interview and thank the committee at the close of the conversation. Remember that the Search Committee will be discussing your candidacy immediately after the phone interview. You want to make a positive impression.

Similarly, the Search Committee must follow federal guidelines for hiring; that is, they must not ask your age; if you are married, have a significant other, or a partner; if you have children; and what race or religion you are. If you bring up a topic, for instance asking about elementary schools in the area, you have opened the door for additional questions about your family situation. How much of your private life you wish to share is up to you. You should give some thought to this issue prior to the interview, so you're not caught off guard.

The On-Campus Interview

Most on-campus interviews take place over a two-day period. Rigorous is the word. You'll be exhausted mentally and physically afterward, as the usually one to two full days of interviewing mean you need to be alert and attentive for up to 12 hours each day. Be polite and gracious to everyone—administrators, faculty, and staff. Express your appreciation to the department secretary who made your travel and scheduling arrangements. Thank your host faculty member(s) who shuttle you from the interview meeting to presentations to meals and to the airport. Upon your arrival back home, write each Search Committee member a handwritten thank-you note.

If you can afford to pay for an extra night's stay, ask the department to arrange for you to spend a couple of hours with a realtor. This will make it appear that if the position is offered to you, you intend to stay at this institution for a period of time and that you are interested in the greater community. More on this later.

Atherton Hall, Pennsylvania State University, State College.

Prior to leaving for the interview, check the weather forecast for the area and dress appropriately. If you are from a warm climate, you may need to borrow a lightweight or even winter coat depending on when and where the interview location may be. If your interview schedule includes a campus tour, that means wear comfortable shoes—and make certain they are clean and polished. Six-inch heels will make it difficult to walk long distances.

Dress for the interview in a comfortable but professional manner. You will wear the same outfit from early morning to late evening, so select something that doesn't show wrinkles. Men can wear a suit or sport coat and tie. The jacket length should be so the bottom of the jacket will meet your cupped hands if you drop your arms to your sides. A navy blue sports coat or a dark suit (charcoal, black, navy, dark brown) is fine for late fall through winter. Spring colors such as a tan suit for men and bright colors for women are fine. Avoid any outfit that will draw the audience to your clothes rather than your presentation—large pinstripes, polka dots, large flowered patterns, a gimmicky tie, and so forth. For women, avoid too short, too low, and too tight. You want your academic message—not your clothing—to be what is remembered by the Search Committee and the administrators you meet.

When you travel to the campus, try to take everything in a carry-on suitcase to eliminate the possibility of lost luggage. The same recommendation applies if you take your own laptop and projector (you may borrow one from your current department) with all the necessary connection cords. Carry both a flash drive of your presentation and copy on your laptop as a backup. Some individuals feel comfortable linking the presentation to their cell phone or as an attachment to an email. Others save theirs in a cloud format they can retrieve offsite. Be aware that some campuses have only Macs, while others have only PCs. You definitely don't want to appear technologically challenged.

During your visit, you'll meet with the Search Committee, Department Chair, Dean or Associate Dean, faculty from the department, and often graduate or undergraduate students. If you are interviewing at a liberal arts or community college, you may also meet with a Vice President of Academic Affairs or Instruction. Some Search Committees meet you for breakfast and will continue to be with you into the evening hours. Generally the meals are at mid-price-range restaurants in the area, but sometimes an evening dinner or gathering may be in the Department Chair's or a faculty member's home. The schedule can be grueling, not because it is intended to be but because it is stressful to represent yourself well throughout an entire day, especially when you are anxious and always on guard to say what is appropriate.

During your interview you will be asked to do a presentation for faculty in the department, usually based on your recent research. Sometimes you will be asked to teach a class of undergraduates or graduates. Information about what is expected of you will be shared with you prior to your visit to allow you to prepare. The Search Committee, the Department Chair, and the Dean of the College will all meet you at various times during the interview period. Depending on the size of the institution, you may also get together with the Department Personnel Committee, which will outline the general requirements to obtain tenure and promotion. An Associate Dean of Research will sometimes be available to talk with you about your grant, research, and scholarship agenda. You will meet with the Search Committee for an exit interview just prior to departing campus. Smaller colleges often have an informal dinner or a gathering at a faculty member's home in the evening.

To prepare for the interview, you need to consider the letter/email of invitation along with the itinerary. Generally the candidate's research topic is the dissertation research study. Be able to deliver a 45-minute presentation and effectively use technology to do so. Any PowerPoint presentation should be well crafted. Each slide should be brief and trigger additional information/concepts that you will provide orally. Slides that contain a paragraph that you then read aloud to the audience result in a boring presentation. If you don't know how to put together a PowerPoint presentation, work with someone to create a polished one. A bit of humor is fine, but don't overdo it. Your message is to present the problem statement, provide a brief overview of the literature review including up-to-date sources (one or two slides), discuss the design of the study, including demographics of the population (if one was used), convey your findings, a link to theorists, and implications for further research in the field. Practice delivering the presentation. Index cards with additional notes are acceptable. Having a handout or a print-out of the PowerPoints for attendees is appropriate. Additionally, consider also bringing a few copies of your CV to hand out for the audience to peruse during your presentation; if the other candidates didn't do this, it will help to set you apart from your competition.

Increasingly, candidates are asked to teach a class, usually at the undergraduate level. The class would typically be one assigned to you if you were offered the position. It's advantageous if you are permitted to select the topic, because it gives you a chance to shine in the class-room. Be sure to use technology and ask for time on the interview day to view and understand the technological devices in the room where you will be teaching. There is nothing worse for your nerves than to sit before a group of students and your evaluators to find you can't get the technology to work. Engage with your student audience and develop rapport. Be creative. Make certain you know the topic inside and out. Chances are undergraduate students won't ask any questions, but faculty in attendance will. Some institutions will consider the input from their students regarding your teaching presentation.

At the end of any group sessions, remember to thank the faculty, administrators, and students for taking time to get to know you and understand what you can bring to the position. The members of Search Committee, in particular, have arranged their schedules to give you their full attention, and they need to be recognized for their efforts.

Keep Your Antennae Up

All hiring has a political dimension. One Dean tried to pacify the departments in his college by annually allocating the same number of new faculty positions to every department regardless of need. Some departments clearly needed additional faculty to meet student demands while other departments had an overabundance of faculty with few classes to teach. Consider the following scenarios: Faculty may openly woo candidates to align with their views on departmental issues; weak faculty may be intimidated by a candidate with a lot of publications or research presentations listed on his/her CV; malcontent faculty may intentionally misrepresent the department and institution. A person in the audience asked one candidate a series of extremely difficult questions during his presentation. The candidate later learned that the individual was an instructor who would lose her position if the candidate was chosen for the job.

Remember, everybody has an agenda. On the one hand, if you notice or sense disagreement about an issue among your interviewers, you can make no comments or, if asked, make positive comments about various perspectives without being obvious about which one you prefer. On the other hand, if an overwhelming majority of faculty favor a particular issue, you may want to make favorable comments as this group of faculty will be inclined to prefer a candidate who favors that same issue.

Administrators are interested in your abilities to teach, conduct research, publish in refereed journals, and bring in grants. They also want someone who will get along with colleagues in the department as well as conduct the routine service—make appropriate updates to curriculum and courses; serve on variety of department, college, and campus committees; and be an advisor to undergraduate and/or graduate students. They will point to the department's and college's mission statements, something you most likely encountered when you visited the university's website.

The Department Chair will share the salary for the position and benefits (dental, health, and life insurance; retirement; etc.) the university provides. There may also be some discussion about the cost of living in the area. Availability of a graduate assistant, lab space, travel funds, and the like will also be shared by the Department Chair. You need to question what part of your work might be considered part of the university's or entirely yours. Generally any royalties from books published are solely the faculty member's. However, if you conduct research and develop a patent, are the financial benefits split 50/50 with the university and you? Are you permitted to serve as a consultant during the academic year? (Typically faculty can serve as consultants during the summer months when they aren't under contract to teach. For instance, chemical engineering faculty may serve as consultants on projects for oil fracking while drama faculty may direct summer stock theater.) The number of courses and amount of release time for research/scholarly activity will most likely be part of this conversation depending on the institution.

What to Ask and Not to Ask

When in doubt, maintain your silence. When you do have questions, always frame those questions in a way that supports your teaching and scholarship efforts and doesn't reflect negatively on your work habits. Examples of typical/acceptable questions include: What are the expectations for tenure and promotion? How many publications or juried art events or recitals are required for tenure? Does advising graduate students and serving on/chairing Thesis and Doctoral Committees count toward tenure? Don't ask how *few* hours you need to devote to meetings or how many days you are required to be on campus each week. Don't ask if you can bring your toddler with you for office hours, but do ask if the university has a child care center (most do or have arrangements with a nearby child care facility).

Do ask about grant writing and technology support. Do new faculty members get a library budget, and a new computer or laptop? Is there assistance available for learning new technology for campus online-course delivery systems or new software? Find out what kind of support is provided for faculty seeking grants. Are there funds available solely for new faculty? Are there workshops for grantsmanship? Is assistance available for creating, budgeting for, and editing grant proposals? Are travel funds provided to meet with grant contacts in Washington, DC?

It is also important to ask how many paper presentations and refereed publications are expected each year. Ask what percentage of the faculty is granted tenure. Be aware that tenure and promotion decisions may vary from department to department within a college. The publishing expectations for the English Department may be quite different than those for the Political Science Department. Lastly, ask how long before a decision will be made on filling the position. This may be particularly helpful to you if you are applying at more than one university, since you would not want to turn down a position while holding out for one that you may not be offered.

Ask about the cost of living in the area, even though you can find much of this information online. You may find the perfect research institution only to learn housing is so expensive you can't afford to live there and have to leave after a year. Also ask the Department Chair if the university assists with relocation expenses. Thus, when arranging your campus visit, ask to meet with a realtor for a half day and indicate that you are willing to pay for an extra night at the hotel.

Maryanne met with a realtor who escorted her around the small university town, showing her housing that assistant professors could generally afford. At one house, the owners were home. After admiring the house Maryanne struck up a conversation with the owners and discovered the owner had worked in the same department in which she had just interviewed but had been denied tenure—as had every other assistant professor—a total of six—in the same college at the university. She felt she was fortunate to have stumbled across this information, which had been kept from her during the interview process. As mentioned above, somewhere in the interview process with the Search Committee you should ask what percentage of the faculty is granted tenure.

At the very least, you can get a perspective from someone outside of the university when you meet with a realtor. Also, you'll learn something about recreational opportunities, the cost of living, and housing possibilities. Some colleges, such as George Mason University, have purchased homes near the institution to rent at a reasonable rate to assistant professors, as housing in the Beltway is very expensive. During informal parts of your interview, you can ask about the community. Be aware that it is important not to stereotype certain expectations related to the diversity in the community. You should have some information from your research, but it is good to hear faculty perspectives. Some Search Committee members may not think you are interested in accepting a position in that city or town if you don't ask some questions about something in the community that you would be looking for in order to feel comfortable.

While the Department Chair will share information about the various retirement benefit options available through the university, also ask the Search Committee members about the retirement options, as they may give you additional insight. The institution provided pension is referred to as "defined retirement benefits." Many states are revising or have already modified their pensions for public employees requiring them to perhaps contribute more to their pension plans or giving more choices in whether to take a state supervised retirement plan or a portable plan from which you may select a variety of stock and bond investments in an annuity that may be taken with you should you leave the institution, hence the term "portable."

In addition to the defined retirement benefits offered by the institution for retirement, you may opt to contribute additional funds to a 403b retirement account (the college version of the 401k that businesses offer their employees) of up to $15,000 per year or $17,500 a year if you are fifty or older. This money is taken monthly out of your paycheck tax free (that is, before federal and state income tax—if any—is taken out) and put into an investment fund such as Fidelity, T. Rowe. Price, TIAA-CREF, or VALIC. The university or college selects the funds to which your 403b may be submitted and you select from the list of vendors they provide. You select which investment fund and the mutual fund(s) to which your monies will go. You sign an agreement so each month a set amount is taken out of your pay and sent by wire to the investment fund on your behalf here it remains there tax free until you start withdrawing it for part of your retirement. The earliest you can start withdrawing without a penalty is when you are 59 1/2. If you don't need it then, you don't have to withdraw anything until you are 70 1/2 years old. Then the portion you withdraw will be taxable.

You should start contributing to a 403b retirement fund when you start at the university. Begin with 5 percent a year (or $3,000 a year on a base salary of $60,000) and then increase your contribution by a percent each time you get a raise of 2 percent or more. By starting when you first are employed, you benefit from "time," because the longer the duration of your investment, the more it will grow tax free in your 403b. A rule of thumb is to put 75 percent of your investment into stocks and 25 percent into bond mutual funds.

Some institutions reward faculty if they stay longer—for instance only paying 5 percent of the institution's retirement commitment until the person has served on the faculty for two or three years, then the full 10 percent thereafter—or even not paying any retirement contribution until you have completed five years at the institution. Do ask how long a person has to work at the university before becoming vested (or qualified) to earn a pension. This may be three to five years in most cases. Should you opt to leave before you are fully vested in the pension system, you may only withdraw the amount of money you contributed to the retirement fund plus interest and get nothing from the university's contributions on your behalf.

Ask about other benefits such as health, dental, vision, life, and long-term care insurance. Does the institution pay for everything for you? Is there a cost reduction for a spouse, significant other, or partner? For children?

Remember, no one from the university can ask you about your family, children, sexual preference, race, or religion during the interview process. If you offer that you want to know the quality of local schools as you have two elementary-age children, however, then they may respond to that question such as by telling you where the better schools are located.

When a Spouse, Significant Other, or Partner Is Also Job Searching

If your spouse, significant other, or partner also is a newly minted or soon-to-be hooded PhD, you may be looking for two positions in the same field at the same time. Many institutions now have provisions upon hiring that make the next opening in the spouse's, significant others, or partner's field available to that person. This option may be included in your job-offer letter at your request.

Sometimes two openings within the same department are available at which point both of you apply. If your spouse, significant other, or partner is in a different field and two appropriate openings are available at an institution, both of you might be interviewed and get the positions only if the fit is good for both departments. If one of you is hired, the other department is not required to hire the spouse, significant other, or partner. Sometimes an institution may offer the spouse, significant other, or partner a job funded by soft money, such as to work on a grant proposals or as an instructor or adjunct assistant professor. Institutions in larger metropolitan areas sometimes assist faculty members in finding positions for their spouse, significant other, or partner at nearby institutions or research centers. Or the two of you can apply for positions in the same locale.

After the Interview

When you arrive home, devote a few minutes to writing hand-written thank-you notes—not emails or text messages—to the members of the Search Committee. Drop them in the mail within three days of your interview. Whether or not you are offered the position, the members of the Search Committee devoted their time to meet with you regarding the opportunity to join them as a colleague, and a note acknowledging their effort is due. As you move on in your university career and become part of a Search Committee yourself, you will realize the importance of running a good and ethical search for the sake of the department, the program, and the candidates who apply.

Now it becomes a waiting game until all the candidates have interviewed and the Search Committee has made its decision and forwards a recommendation of one or two names to the Department Chair. In some institutions, the Search Committee makes the final decision, while in others the Department Chair makes the selection with input from the Search Committee. Still other institutions have the Dean make the final decision. Typically the input of the faculty at large is also a part of the decision-making process. Generally they are asked to fill out an evaluation form after your interview has been completed. This information is given to the Search Committee, whose members will appreciate faculty input to help them make their decision.

Once the Department Chair has the final approval to offer the position from the Dean and the Provost, the call to the candidate is made. The Department Chair will offer a salary and give a deadline as to when the candidate—you—have to let the university know. This is a time for additional negotiations. Most institutions will offer funds for travel to present at conferences, for lab or studio materials, and for library materials, which may be more generous for first-year instructors, or until you gain tenure, than for instructors who are already tenured. One faculty member was able to get additional space for her library of books. During the negotiation period you can counter the institution's offer by requesting a higher salary, a graduate assistant, more desirable office space, a better research lab, or a reduction in teaching load for the first year or two. Always remember that your future salary will be based on your first-year's salary. Hence, it is important to try to get as much money as you possibly can during your negotiations. This negotiation period is typically short—two weeks or less. Sometimes, even after the negotiations have been concluded, you may ask for an additional small item.

Roles of Administrators

The arrival of new faculty translates into new ideas and energy. Ideally, the new faculty member will arrive with a research agenda and publishable dissertation findings while also having in hand an acceptance of a presentation for an upcoming national or regional conference. But first, the interview process must occur.

The justification for the new faculty position is typically written by the Department Chair, who shares it with the Dean and, in many cases, other Department Chairs within the college. The Dean, if he or she approves the need for the position, then takes it to the Provost for final approval. Approval from the Provost means that the department has been issued a faculty line, which some universities designate with a number and a specific salary amount. Once the faculty position is approved, the Department Chair works with the Search Committee to write an ad, describing not only the faculty position with its requirements and preferred qualifications for the job but a generic overview of the college and the university itself. The university then posts an ad for the position on professional organization listserves, in the *Chronicle of Higher Education,* and in other field-appropriate publications. The sooner in the fall semester the ad appears the greater the likelihood of having a large, high-quality applicant pool.

Forming the Search Committee

The Department Chair assigns individuals to the Search Committee. Some universities will have appointed one member from outside the department, while other institutions have all the committee members from the department. Usually there is an attempt to have a diverse committee. In addition, one committee member is usually a student, either graduate or undergraduate. One faculty member, usually tenured, will chair the committee. Sometimes there may be Co-Chairs. All members should know what the demands and expectations are for the position.

One concern in creating a Search Committee is always having faculty serve who have a personal agenda. Another issue is having committee members who are willing to not only put in the many hours it takes but also be flexible to meet so the search is not delayed. The Search Committee should be balanced in terms of gender, experience, and race if possible. Certainly the area in which the new faculty member will teach should be well represented.

Affirmative Action Requirements

The Department Chair and the Dean must make certain that affirmative action rules and regulations are followed, and that the search is not contaminated in any manner. This usually requires that all Search Committee members receive training by the affirmative action officer for the university, and that this training is recorded and kept on file in the department or the Dean's office. Generally, this training must be taken every two years by an administrator such as a Department Chair or a Dean or if a faculty member is to serve on a Search Committee. The training includes knowing the proper protocols of conducting job interviews, such as providing similar lodging and meal arrangements for each candidate during his/her campus visit and making sure schedules allot the same amount of time for each candidate's presentation and interviews with the Department Chair, Dean, Search Committee, and Department Personnel Committee.

Also covered will be what questions may and may not legally be asked without infringing on the rights of the applicant, and other pertinent guidelines. Only appropriate questions can be asked that relate to the job position itself. Any questions regarding, race, religious beliefs, age, gender, sexual orientation, or family are considered inappropriate and violate federal Equal Employment Opportunity guidelines.

Allowing an application submitted late to be reviewed is inappropriate unless the search has been formally reopened as per affirmative action guidelines. Notes relating to the discussions of the committee must be kept and filed in a secure location until the search is successfully completed, then shredded.

Search Committee Duties

Serving as a member of the Search Committee is an important role for any faculty member. The majority of Search Committee members will have expertise in the field for which the candidate has applied so they will familiar with leaders in the area and publications to some extent. Some will have read one or two of the applicant's publications prior to his/her campus visit, if the applicant is already published prior to the interview.

The Search Committee meets several times as an entire body with every member present (or included in a conference call) during the course of the interview process. Maintaining confidentiality is a key element of serving on a Search Committee. No aspect of the search deliberations can be revealed. Phone calls to references, ranking of candidates, even knowledge of who applied or who didn't cannot be revealed to anyone outside of the Search Committee except for the Department Chair and Dean, the latter two at the conclusion of the deliberations by the Search Committee. This is essential so the search is valid and not contaminated. The Chair of the Search Committee may report that the pool is small and request colleagues in the department contact individuals they know at other institutions to try to encourage more applications. Faculty at large might be asked to take brochures to conferences or email the job posting to leaders in the field.

Each Search Committee member gets to review all of the completed applications and rank them. Some members may review them as the applications come in while others may wait until a few days before the final due date. Sharing perspectives about each applicant and weighing the strengths and weaknesses as they pertain to the job description is part of the task. Then the Search Committee narrows the number of applicants to a pool of six to ten top candidates. Every applicant who meets the position's minimum qualifications (as advertised) initially goes into this pool. For instance, an applicant who possesses a master's degree but who won't complete the doctorate until the next academic year, after the time frame stipulated in the ad for the position, would not meet the requirements. If someone has taught one year in an American school when the position requires a minimum of three years, that individual would fail to meet requirements, and so on.

Next, the applicant pool is narrowed by including those who possess the additional qualifications as defined in the position ad, such as experience teaching at the university level, and so on. Note that the committee may continue to include any or all of the individuals who have the minimal position requirements. Any applicant who is removed from the pool must have a verified reason that he/she does not meet requirements. Otherwise, the applicant must remain in the pool of candidates.

Each Search Committee member then separately evaluates the pool of candidates. Evaluations of the research and teaching presentations are collected and taken into consideration by the Search Committee. In effect the candidate is being sized up to see if he/she holds potential in teaching at the university level and of putting his/her research agenda together to become a noted scholar in the field. The Search Committee may then rank the candidates as to which ones would be invited to engage in a phone interview.

The committee creates a set of questions to be asked of the references provided by the candidates as well as those asked of the candidates during phone interviews and then during on-campus formal interviews.

The Phone Interview

For each candidate, a sheet listing the name of the individual, institution from which he/she earned his/her doctoral degree, the title of the candidate's dissertation, and his/her related work experiences should be prepared so that each Search Committee member will have a quick reference. Below this section should be the questions to be asked during the phone interview with ample room for the Search Committee member to jot notes of the applicant's response under the question. The questions must be refined, in writing, and asked word for word of each phone candidate. See the sample phone interview sheet below.

Sample of Phone Interview Sheet

Name of Candidate: _____

Institution of Doctoral Degree: _____

Defense Date: _____

Dissertation Title: _____

Date of Phone Interview: _____

Questions:

1. **What attracted you to this position?**

2. **What skills do you possess that you believe make you a good fit for this position?**

3. **Who are the noted leaders in the field that influence your research?**

4. **What do you believe may be the next major trend or finding in your field?**

5. **Five years from now, where do you expect to be in your career?**

6. **What is a question you expected us to ask that we didn't?**

7. **Are there any questions that you have for the Search Committee?**

Phone interviews, which are generally last thirty- to forty-five-minute conference calls with the entire Search Committee, are used to screen out candidates so only those with the best talents and fit for the position are brought to campus. The committee members introduce themselves and tell a bit about their role in the department such as what they teach, their committee involvement, research interests, and so forth. Then a set of questions (such as those above) are asked, usually with the Search Committee members taking turns. At the conclusion of the phone interview, the candidate is asked if there are any questions that he/she might like to ask the Search Committee.

After each candidate's phone interview, fifteen minutes should be provided for the Search Committee to review the candidate's responses. Additional notes may be taken during this discussion. Did the candidate respond with clarity and thoughtfulness? Or was there a hesitation? Were some responses off task?

After all the phone interviews have been conducted, the Search Committee must narrow the applicant list. At this point, this number of applicants may depend upon what the administration has indicated to be a viable number of candidates to be brought on campus. Sometimes only two candidates may be brought in while other departments and universities may bring in five candidates. If finances for candidate travel are an issue, an extra candidate who lives within driving distance of the university may be invited to interview.

The On-Campus Interview

The interview schedule must take into consideration the travel plans of the candidates. It is important to avoid travel that is too early or too late in the day just to protect the budget for the search, when this timing can be disadvantageous for the candidate. To have a candidate arrive late at night and expect the candidate to be prepared for an early breakfast, a presentation, and a meeting with the Dean early in the day is unfair. Also, there needs to be a buffer so candidates for the same position won't encounter each other in the hallways.

A number of faculty, both Search Committee members and other members of the department, should share the duties of hosting meals, picking up candidates at the hotel, and giving a campus tour. So much can be learned about a candidate's abilities and personality during informal encounters. For example, the conversation during the drive to and from the hotel is often revealing for Search Committee members, because the candidate might express information not covered in the formal interview process or a Search Committee member might get the chance to ask the candidate to expand on a particular topic. A silent ride from or to the hotel does not bode well for the candidate.

Search Committee members should not discuss salary, technology availability, laboratory or art studio arrangements, travel funds, and other benefits with the candidates. If a department has a standard procedure for new faculty such as an extra course release or providing a graduate assistant for ten hours a week, that information may be shared.

The on-campus schedule should take into account a reasonable amount of time to move from one event to another. Often finding the time for the candidate to fit into the Dean's or the Associate Dean's schedule is challenging; however, no Dean should delegate the responsibility of formally interviewing every faculty candidate. It is too important for the college to do so.

The Interview Process

All faculty in the department need to be alerted in advance about on-campus interviews. Having the same, set schedule for each candidate

---

Sample On-Campus Interview Schedule

John Maxwell, ABD
University of Texas

Wednesday, February 12

Arrive via Flight 1212 at 3:30 PM and take Murphy's Limo (888-654-3210) to campus. Check in at University Suites

6:00 PM dinner with Dr. Mark Latos, Department Chair (will pick Candidate up in front of hotel)

Thursday, February 13

7:00 AM	Breakfast with Dr. Carol Owens, Chair, Search Committee (will pick Candidate up in front of hotel and bring to campus after breakfast)
8:30 AM	Research presentation by Candidate to Search Committee members in Fairmont Hall 321
9:30 AM	Meet with Associate Dean, Research, in Fairmont Hall 434
10:00 AM	Break
10:20 AM	Meet with Dean Susan Votto in Fairmont Hall 432
11:00 AM	Teaching presentation to undergraduates Fairmont Hall 121
11:45 AM	Break
12:00 PM	Lunch and campus tour with Graduate Students (will escort candidate to Student Center)
1:15 PM	Meet with Department Personnel Committee in Fairmont Hall 321
2:00 PM	Meet with Department Chair, Dr. Latos, in Fairmont Hall 344
2:45 PM	Meet with Search Committee in Fairmont Hall 321
3:30 PM	Pick up by Limo to take to airport for Flight 2131 departing at 5:45 PM

(i.e., holding the candidate's research presentation at 10:00 for each candidate and in the same conference room but on different days) should help faculty arrange their schedules to attend most of the research and teaching presentations, thereby garnering a large attendance. Email reminders should be sent to faculty the day before the candidates' visits. Some departments make posters to inform faculty of the visit, and such a display serves to welcome the applicant for that day.

Search Committee members should be reminded to keep to the itinerary and to meet the time expectations. Any special requests by a candidate such as to preview the technology or the lab, and so forth, need to be ironed out no later than noon the day prior to the visit—Friday morning if the interview begins on Sunday evening. Committee members must present themselves as organized and collegial.

Sometimes Search Committee members forget that the interview process is a two-way street—the candidate is sizing up the faculty just as they are evaluating the prospects of having the candidate aboard as a colleague. Professional appearance and manner is required during the on campus visit. The candidate should be escorted to the various meetings, holding to the time schedule outlined. During dinner, don't share horror stories about funding cuts that took place a decade ago or the bizarre-acting Department Chair who left abruptly five years ago; on the other hand, don't paint an overly rosy picture of the department. As the old police show advocated, "Just the facts" should be shared. Don't embellish. Just be *professionally* honest. When a potential new colleague later discovers all is not what it seemed to be, that person may likely move on to another institution.

Like Search Committee members, administrators need to maintain confidentiality. The Department Chair or the Dean shouldn't reveal the salary offer in front of a member of the Search Committee. Nor should the Department Chair brag to the Dean, other Chairs, or faculty that the candidate was hired at a bargain-basement salary.

Interviews with respective administrators need to be formal, but the candidate should be put at ease. It will put the candidate's mind at ease if the administrator is professional and open to discussion, especially if the candidate is leaving a prior position due to lack of respect for an administrator, which is often a reason for leaving another institution. A cold or threatening undertone gives the wrong impression. A checklist of items to be discussed helps prevent an item from being inadvertently omitted as well as helps keep the interview process on task and makes the interviewee feel that it is a professional process.

Conclusion

The search process requires research and commitment from the candidate, members of the Search Committee, and administrators. Search Committees need to select those applicants to be interviewed who best meet the department's needs. Candidates should be serious about the position if they accept the invitation to interview on campus. The Department Chair and the Dean need to make certain a level playing field is established and to encourage department faculty to attend the presentations by the candidates and offer their impressions. The more input, the more informed the hiring decision becomes and the more relaxed everyone will be when the candidate arrives on campus as a new faculty member.

Since candidates are applying simultaneously to other institutions, the longer the search process is drawn out, the greater the likelihood that candidates will take positions at other institutions. Also, the earlier the search process begins in the fall may result in some candidates applying solely to hone their interviewing skills before the primary search season begins.

Epilogue

Over the years the authors have collected numerous interview stories from faculty at universities across the United States and Canada. Here are some scenarios shared with us. We have modified the scenarios slightly so the actual institution and individuals involved are not recognizable.

Scenario One: Wardrobe Malfunction

Rita left work and drove directly to the airport for her flight to a university three states away. She brought her briefcase, with her research presentation on a flash drive along with an ample supply of handouts, on the plane with her, but she checked her other bag and waited for the plane to depart. On the flight she reviewed her notes, confident that she could deliver the presentation in her sleep. A late afternoon flight, the gentleman next to her purchased a small bottle of Jim Beam and promptly spilled part of it on her slacks. The man apologized, and Rita shrugged it off.

Upon landing, Rita discovered that her checked bag had been placed on the wrong flight but was assured that it would be delivered by the next day. She took a limo to the hotel, spruced herself up as much as she could under the circumstances, and went out to dinner with a few members of the Search Committee and shared the story of the incident on the plane. A few minutes later, the waiter spilled a glass of red wine on her. Now she reeked of alcohol and had wine stains on her only set of clothing and; at this late hour, it was too late to go to a department store or mall to get another outfit.

The next day, Rita was stuck wearing the now stained outfit she had worn to work the day before. At the end of the interview day, two members of the Search Committee were putting her in the airport limo when a van pulled up delivering her lost bag.

A few days later, Rita got a call from the Department Chair offering her the position, which she accepted. Several months after she had been at the university she asked a member of the Search Committee why they had offered her the job when she smelled of alcohol and certainly wasn't dressed professionally. The faculty member replied, "Well, we did give you a lot of points for flexibility."

Scenario Two: More Than I Wanted to Know

Trev had had a great interview. He felt the faculty and Department Chair wanted him and seemed receptive to his ideas. By dinner he was quite pleased with how the interview had gone. Three members of the Search Committee made small talk as they waited for their dinner orders to arrive. During a pause, Trev decided to ask a question to break the silence. "What's it like working with the Department Chair?" One senior faculty member leaned across the table and gave a twenty-five-year history of all the incompetent Chairs the department had had, ending with the fact that the last three had been fired, one after a single year in the position. The question Trev had asked clearly related to the current Chair who was never mentioned and who had been in the Chair position for four years.

Scenario Three: Am I Not Welcomed?

It is the custom at most universities to have a welcome placard outside of the college lobby announcing the interview of "Dr. John Jones" for a particular departmental position. It is a good feeling to see that the department is prepared and looking forward to the candidate's visit. Two other departments in the same building were also interviewing candidates. There were, however, only two welcome placards, and three candidates. The candidate, Jeanette Adams, noticed that she did not have a welcome placard. She read the other two and made a decision not to say anything about her not being welcomed in a similar fashion as the other two candidates. It crossed her mind to make a joke about how she is not welcomed, but she chose to remain silent. It would not be a positive start to the interview because it would make the department look unprepared. She made a good decision not to bring it up. It is never good to bring up a shortcoming of the institution, even when it is obvious. It is fine, however, to make it play into your final decision on accepting a position at one institution over another.

Scenario Four: In Sight but Out of Mind

Deborah's interview was on a bright spring day. Pleased to be able to stretch her legs on a campus tour, she headed out with a young assistant professor as her tour guide. Before they even reached the door, the assistant professor made a call on her cell phone and proceeded to engage in a phone conversation as they walked around campus until they returned to the building from which they had come. Deborah had been leaning toward taking the position, yet when the Chair called and offered it, she declined, explaining that she felt the faculty weren't interested in her.

Scenario Five: Misreading the Search Committee

Eugene had a great interview and was excited about the position. He thought he related well to the Search Committee and Department Chair. In fact, the Chair of the Search Committee told him as he got into the limo to leave that the committee had met and recommended that he be selected—something rarely done by a Search Committee. After two weeks of not hearing from the university, Eugene was concerned. He'd canceled an interview with another university as he thought he had the job at University A. After three weeks, he received a letter from

University A's Department Chair saying the position had been filled and wishing him luck. Months later Eugene discovered that the Dean had overridden both the Department Chair's and the Search Committee's wishes to hire Eugene, because they wanted someone with more credentials. Fortunately, Eugene ended up with a position at another institution, but he now advises his own doctoral students to make certain the job offer is in writing and so is the acceptance from the interviewee.

Scenario Six: Accepting a Position

Emma had lined up several interviews but wasn't having much success during the fall and early spring in attaining a position. Finally in late April, she was offered a position at a medium-size university. She wrote her letter of acceptance and was set to go there. A week later, Emma received an invitation to interview at another institution—which she accepted. Emma loved the institution and the feeling was mutual. Emma received an offer a few days after her interview, and she accepted the position. She never bothered to notify the first institution, despite receiving emails and phone messages. Emma even changed her cell phone number. A few months after the fall semester began, Emma was having dinner with a colleague at a conference. Seated at the next table were two members of the Search Committee from the institution she spurned. The lack of professionalism followed Emma as word spread in her organization that she accepted a position and then backed out without notification. The first university could have held Emma to her contract if its Department Chair and legal counsel had so wished.

Opposite page: Moseley Hall, Bowling Green State University, Bowling Green, Ohio.

2

Carving Out an Academic Career

Upon your arrival at your new academic institution as a new faculty member, you will be making decisions—which classes and which sections of classes you prefer to teach, which days you'd like to be on campus, when you would like to have lab or studio hours, and the like. You may even be given a choice of which office you'd prefer, with the window offices being the prime real estate in the department. It may be that your office will be painted the color of your choice and new furniture added if you are lucky. Other situations may mean you have to go over to the furniture and equipment storage facility owned by the university and locate a usable desk, chair, bookcases, side table, and other useful items. In good economic times, such furniture can be somewhat plush, but in economic downturns the available goods may be scratched, damaged, or worn out.

Upon settling in and arranging your office, make it pleasant—as you will be spending lots of hours each week there. Consider, if you do have a window, if you want it beside you or positioned so you look directly outside. How accessible is the printer—or is there a remote printer for the department? If your side chair is overly comfortable students and colleagues will find it pleasant to drop by and chat. One faculty member had a folding chair as a side chair to discourage long, lingering chats that ate up his research and writing time. Shelve your books by the author's last name and in areas of topics so you won't be wasting time searching for a missing title. Loaning books to students may result in the books being returned years later once the students have moved out of their apartment or house—if they get returned at all.

Teaching

Course selection will obviously depend on your area of expertise. One candidate in a search indicated that she wanted to write a new doctoral course in poetry, which she loved and preferred not to teach undergraduates. She didn't get the position. The more flexible you are in teaching courses can be a two-edge sword: If you can teach a variety of courses within your department, you'll probably be a favorite of your Department Chair, but you'll have less time to write, conduct research, and the like due to the need to constantly prep for the courses and keep up to date. It is advantageous to develop new courses in line with your expertise. Such work is looked upon favorably in the department annual reviews and can be very satisfying professionally as an instructor.

Developing curricula via adding new courses or revamping current courses also falls under teaching. Often the accreditation of programs results in changes to courses or the program of study as modifications and new advancements in a field of study are addressed by the accreditation body. This is a great opportunity for junior faculty to contribute and to enhance their curriculum vitae.

In higher education, fields are always evolving. As new theories and research findings emerge, departments and majors change and are modified. This results in new courses to be developed and taught at both the undergraduate and graduate levels. Course ideas may come up through discussions with colleagues at other institutions or by perusing curricula of other programs at peer institutions.

Teaching also covers serving on Master's and Doctoral Committees, either as a committee member or as Chair. Such committee work demonstrates that you nurture young researchers in your field of study. Co-presenting research papers or coauthoring peered reviewed manuscripts serves to introduce the neophyte graduate student into your field as well as to advance your own professional career.

Teaching at a small liberal arts institution may mean that you are teaching four classes a semester—all different preparations. If there is a winter term, you may have to teach during that period as well for a total of twenty-four to twenty-seven credit hours of course work in an academic year.

As mentioned earlier, most small liberal arts institutions place greater importance on teaching than on the scholarly productivity that mid- to large-size institutions tend to emphasize. It is possible to attain tenure and promotion at a small liberal arts college, for instance, with perhaps as few as one or two refereed journal articles and two or three professional presentations. At a large research institution, you may have

Creighton's west mall, Creighton University, Omaha, Nebraska.

publish six to eight refereed journal articles in noted journals within your field and present papers at two or three major conferences during the academic year. Large institutions may also provide graduate or teaching assistants as well as a modest teaching load of one to two courses per semester with nothing over winter break for a total teaching load of six to twelve hours during the year. However, budget cuts are making heavier course teaching loads more commonplace across institutions.

For each semester and for each course you teach, note which assignments worked and which need to be modified, revised, or dropped. Find out from other colleagues in your department which assignment they found to be effective, which articles and chapters were well suited for students to read, which new textbooks in the field have a good fit for the course and the students who take it.

It is important to make certain that each course covers what it is supposed to cover. Faculty who teach higher level courses find it frustrating to discover that a key component from an introductory course was never covered by a colleague. And it is even worse if it occurs over and over again, semester after semester. That's why course syllabi with specific objectives are written and adopted by faculty in the first place. Some faculty use "academic freedom" as a cover for failing to include all the assignments and readings on the departmental course syllabi. However, a course syllabus is a contract between the university and the student.

Presenting Papers at Professional Conferences

As travel costs increase, particularly conference registration fees, faculty are finding they need to pay a larger portion of the cost out of their own pocket to attend conferences. Most colleges and universities will only pay for faculty to attend a conference if they present, as only presentations in which the individual is listed in the conference program can be recorded on annual reviews and for tenure and/or promotion. Further complicating the issue, you need to submit proposals to present your research papers about nine months in advance of when the conference takes place so that they can be reviewed in a blind review process. Hence you need to send out several conference proposals in hopes at least one is accepted each year.

Some colleges and universities are modifying their requirements for scholarship in terms of presentations at conferences. However, you need to make certain the requirements appear in writing as an official stance of the department, college, and university at large and not just mentioned in a faculty meeting. Also if the Department Chair changes during your six-year period for which you are preparing to go up for tenure and promotion, what one Department Chair may agree to the new Chair may not. Only the approved, written faculty guidelines are those used for merit pay and promotion to full professor.

Professional conferences enable you to attend presentations by the highest level researchers and theorists in your field. You can also network, introduce yourself to colleagues in the field, and often become part of research studies or a contributor of a chapter in a book by engaging in firsthand meetings with your professional peers at conferences and after hours at cocktail parties and dinners. Some departments hold gatherings to spotlight their doctoral students and faculty, sending out invitations via email prior to the conference.

If it is your goal to become a nationally recognized scholar, you need to be familiar with current scholars in the field. Conferences tend to be where research is first disseminated, so it is important that you be in the audience.

Scholarly Productivity

Having a defined research agenda helps to keep you on target. That said, you may not want to spend your entire career studying the same general topic you pursued in your dissertation. New fields of research open, and you may find jumping in the midst of new ideas stimulates your mind and broadens opportunities. A general rule is to research, write, and present in your field—and not in some latent area of interest that you want to dabble in. If your field is English, don't write articles about remodeling and flipping houses for a profit. You won't get credit for jumping the fence to put it mildly. Stay put in your academic field and make worthwhile contributions to it.

The basic requirement of an academic career is to have a steady research agenda in which you can produce papers accepted for presentations at major conferences in your field and that you can revise to submit to refereed journals. Consistency over a long period of time is far better than having three national presentations and two refereed articles in two years followed by a drought of three years—an inconsistency that looks quite conspicuous on your curriculum vitae. You are constructing your academic career and need to demonstrate that you are progressing by getting published in increasingly more rigorous journals and obtaining larger and more lucrative grants.

Critical to your success as a faculty member is to present and publish your work in what the department values. Some departments or fields value papers presented at major research conferences and expect two such presentations for each academic year. Other fields may value paper presentations and refereed articles in leading professional journals. Still other fields may require book chapters. The fields of English and History often judge the scholarly work of faculty by the publication of books in their field and how they are critiqued in book reviews and who the reviewers are. Artists and musicians are often evaluated by reviews of their artistic endeavors in shows or invitations to present at other universities.

In some cases, you may have to choose what type of scholarly productivity to pursue. Take a book, for example. After locating a publisher willing to publish the work, only one of three book contracts are ever fulfilled—meaning that there are number faculty who fully intend to produce a long academic work but only a third of those who set out actually complete the book and get it to the bookshelf. Some departments may view a book as having the same weight as an article in a refereed journal in the field—despite the obvious greater amount of effort and time to produce a book. The reasons for this vary: It may be the basic nature of the field itself, or it may be that faculty within the department don't want to set the bar higher, thereby making it a requirement that all faculty write a book in order to attain tenure and promotion, even though the university guidelines may indicate that books are to be given more weight than articles and book chapters. Still others prefer not to have to adhere to a standard themselves by acknowledging a peer's effort in publishing a much longer work than an article. Others may resent the financial success or acclaim that a peer might receive for such a work.

The topic of the book itself can be an issue. If you are a faculty member in the Art Department, you may elect to write a niche book on a very specific area of art. Someone in Geology may decide not only to research and publish articles but to write an introductory textbook. A faculty member in the English Department might write a novel. An education faculty member might decide to write methods books that teachers can use to develop lessons for their students. A psychologist may write a pop culture book. The work itself will be scrutinized by the Department Chair and the Department Personnel Committee in the annual review, third-year review, and tenure/promotion papers. Starting a book and then stopping after a few chapters have been written can be expensive as you've lost valuable time that could have been used to conduct research and write several articles or presentations at conferences. Starting a book and seeing it through to its publication can be extremely rewarding within your department and field. Colleagues at other institutions may latch on to it and use it with their own students. Good recommendations bring notoriety to you and your institution—admirable for both.

Colleagues Inside and Outside the Department

During your first week on campus, start developing collegial relationships with other faculty within your department. These should include faculty across the range of experience. Senior, tenured faculty are most apt to serve on the Department Personnel Committee. You need the support of more junior faculty within your department as they may become your career-long confidants should you elect to stay at the institution. Often when you are hired at the same time as another faculty member, a natural collegial bond occurs. If you are in the situation where no one was hired with you or not until a couple of years later, you can feel pretty much alone but confident that your likelihood of getting tenure and promotion is good given the lack of comparison to the work of others.

Writing grants with colleagues can be a way to achieve two things: a new skill in writing grant proposals and a close working relationship with a colleague either within or outside your department. Increasingly, budget issues make grant writing a very favored quality for faculty to possess. As budgets get even tighter, this will likely continue.

Forming or Joining a Writing Group

Just like having an exercise buddy, a writing buddy or group may motivate you to higher levels. You may not believe your work is worthy of a top-notch journal until someone in the writing group points out that your work is just what the editor had in mind when a call for manuscripts went out. A writing group can foster competition, which can be good—or bad—depending on your personality. Also a writing group can help you develop your writing skills—something every new assistant professor can use. Lastly, the comradery of meeting for lunch for a couple of hours every couple of weeks and discussing topics in your field bodes well for stretching you as a researcher and writer plus gives you a feeling of being part of the academic community within your department. And that is very good.

Typically writing groups establish a timetable of submissions by the various members via email, Dropbox, etc., with the other members writing a critique of both positive and negative comments, which are turned over to the author of the manuscript. The writing group is a good way to submit trial balloons of potential research studies as well as to discuss a research design. Oftentimes you'll discover a colleague with a similar research or writing interest that may evolve into a long-term collegial relationship. For instance Richard and Charley discovered they had a similar love of assessment and wrote a textbook together that went into several editions before they retired.

Service

It is difficult to nail down exactly how many committees of what specific type you should serve on for tenure and promotion. Some departments encourage serving on one department, one college, and one university committee each year. This can be troublesome, as many committee positions are filled by an election process. Some allow only tenured faculty to serve. Others are voluntary and may not count as much as elected committee positions. Usually departments don't restrict the number of committees on which an individual can serve. In such a case, one faculty member may serve on six or seven committees while another serves on only one or two. If the department has merit pay, every faculty member will need to have a strong service record in order to receive credit for committee work.

If service includes committee work outside the institution, it is critical to volunteer to serve on committees and boards within your professional memberships. This may mean getting a mentor outside of your institution who can introduce you to various leaders in your organization. Oftentimes this is done by your dissertation Chair. Or you can simply introduce yourself at a cocktail party at the end of a day of conference presentations. It doesn't hurt to be proactive. Developing a professional base of colleagues in your field is critical to becoming well-known and respected. Keep in mind there is a difference between introducing yourself and being pushy with your own agenda. The latter can leave a bad impression that may last for years.

Roles of Administrators

The new faculty member needs mentoring—even if that individual came in at a senior rank of associate or full professor. It is vital that a good match be made when the Department Chair selects a mentor for that individual. For instance, one Chair assigned an inexperienced assistant professor to mentor an associate professor, which proved to be a total mismatch for both. Another Department Chair assigned a narcissistic associate professor to mentor a very competent new assistant professor who quickly resented the "airs" put on by the associate professor.

The Department Chair should play the role of nurturer from afar in the sense that as Chair, certain supportive measures can be taken to assist the new faculty member. This includes providing additional funds for presenting at conferences; for needed technology, lab space, and/or support for research; for research seed projects, and the like. Care must be given not to provide a freshman group of assistant professors with more assistance and support than the sophomore class of assistant professors received. This could give the newer assistant professors an unfair advantage in the tenure and promotion process.

Deans must make certain that new faculty feel welcome and they receive the necessary assistance both from within their respective departments and from the college itself. The beginning of the semester speeches should start and end on a positive note to convey that good things are happening within the college. Deans should invite new assistant professors as well as second-year assistant professors to have either a lunch or a breakfast a couple of times during the academic year so the new faculty can share experiences. For instance, just knowing a slightly more senior faculty member is helpful in learning about how to complete a travel voucher after presenting at a conference or how to use the annual review template for reporting teaching, scholarly productivity, and service reviews.

Overview Likelihood of Gaining Promotion to Full Professor

A recent study was conducted by the American Historical Association considering History faculty tenure rates. A survey of over 2,200 tenure-track History faculty members at U.S. colleges and universities found that married men tended to gain promotion to full professor in 5.9 years while single men took an average of 6.4 years. For women, the case was much different. Female historians who were married or had been married at the time of the survey took an average of 7.8 years to progress in rank from associate to full professor. Those who were single and never married at the time of the survey reported taking only 6.7 years to be promoted from associate to full professor. Indeed, female full professors were more likely to never have married at all and were twice as likely to list their marital status as divorced or separated (Coe, 2013).

EPILOGUE

Scenario One: Your Productivity Makes Your Colleagues Jealous

Jonathan was a type "A" personality. Professor Workaholic could have been his name. His department was top-heavy with male faculty whose productivity had declined over the years. His Chair was new and quite insecure. She felt Jonathan was likely to challenge her for the Chair position in a few years. Jonathan was shocked to get a low evaluation on his second-year faculty contributions, as he had published as many articles and made as many peer reviewed presentations of research papers as anyone in the department. Students flocked to his classes, and he'd been appointed by the Dean and Provost to two important university committees. When he complained to the Dean that the Department Chair and faculty in the department were jealous of his success, the Dean told him to just stop what he was doing. Jonathan said he couldn't. He valued his research and enjoyed teaching and serving on commit-tees. The Dean replied, "Exactly. You can either choose to cut back so no one is jealous of your productivity and teaching or continue to be highly productive." Jonathan then decided to devote even more energy to publishing, service, and teaching, which resulted in top ratings given by the Personnel Committee and a larger amount of merit pay each year. He was given tenure and promotion but then left for another position at another institution that paid less but had a more collegial atmosphere in the department.

Scenario Two: Your Mentor Leaves Unexpectedly

Charlene enjoyed working with her mentor, Jeanne. They shared a similar philosophy about their field and often collaborated on manuscripts and presentations at professional conferences. However, at the end of Charlene's second year as an assistant professor, Jeanne unexpectedly resigned to take a Chair position at another institution. While Charlene was pleased for her mentor, she was alarmed at no longer having Jeanne to nurture her as they seemed a perfect pair of senior/junior colleagues. Because Charlene was doing everything at that point to get tenure and promotion in terms of her teaching, scholarly productivity, and service, the Department Chair didn't appoint anyone to serve as her mentor. While Jeanne still emailed and followed Charlene on Facebook, after a few months that stopped as well. Charlene felt abandoned and unable to function. Her teaching began declining. She made excuses regarding her research and writing commitments. She attended committee meetings but contributed little. Charlene finally went to her doctor who diagnosed her as being depressed. He urged her to seek out someone at her institution whom she could trust as a colleague. Charlene ultimately got tenure and promotion but never regained the initial spark she had as a beginning assistant professor.

Scenario Three: Salary Inequities

Bill and Rita had been hired the same year. Three years later, two more faculty members were hired. Rumors in the department were that the new faculty members were making more money than Bill and Rita. The following fall, Bill and Rita went to the university library information desk and asked to see the salaries of faculty within their college. Since the university was a public university, salaries are public information and anyone can make such a request under federal public information laws. Bill and Rita learned that the rumors were correct. The new faculty members were making $7,000 a year more than they were. They went back to the department and tried to encourage other faculty members to join them in complaining to their Chair. However, their colleagues were sympathetic but not interested in causing upheaval in the department and college. They wrote a letter to their Department Chair and copied the Dean and the Provost. Two years later, a salary study was made within the university, and salary adjustments were made over a three-year period that gave both Bill and Rita about $5,000 more in salary. Still Bill and Rita felt they had been deprived for years of the additional increments that the newer faculty had received.

Scenario Four: Colleagues Who Are Unethical

Susan slaved evenings and weekends working on her research. When she remarked to her colleague, also a nontenured faculty member, he remarked that he wrote with his doctoral students so he was able to produce more papers for conferences and articles in journals. Such professional collaboration is perfectly acceptable. Susan thought that was a great idea and pursued it. However, when Susan lunched with Mary, a colleague in a different department, she learned that some faculty use the "favor" approach, putting names of colleagues on their article submissions even though those faculty had not contributed to the work in any manner. If the article would be published, then the other individuals would "owe" that faculty member a publication or paper presentation. Mary was frustrated by this practice, which she viewed as being unethical and eventually found a position at another institution.

Scenario Five: Balancing Teaching, Scholarship, and Service

Katie found her first year as an assistant professor mentally and physically exhausting. She worked hard to prepare her classes, serve dutifully on committees, and write manuscripts and submit them based on her dissertation research. But Katie found a way to be better organized—she compartmentalized her time. She reworked and honed her syllabi during two full weeks each summer—using notes she'd made the previous fall and spring semesters of teaching and in content cadre meetings for her courses within her department. During the academic year she served on committees but limited them to one at each level on campus—department, college, and university—and two in her professional organizations. She conducted research during the fall and spring semesters, then used six weeks during each summer to write up the results. During the academic year she met twice a month with colleagues in a writing critique group. This still gave her a month each summer to travel to visit relatives and friends and stay fresh and energized.

By compartmentalizing time and carefully managing her schedule, Katie was able to become a top-notch instructor, develop into a well-known and nationally recognized scholar, and be a respected colleague on committees over the years.

Opposite page: Carnegie Library, DePauw University, Greencastle, Indiana.

3

Welcome to Your New Ivory Tower
The First Year

Now that you have chosen the institution, what comes next? It is time to move closer to your entrance into the Ivory Tower.

Being the brand new faculty member is challenging. The expectations are high as is the learning curve for understanding the department's and college's culture. Your goal is to settle in and work toward gaining tenure and promotion. Tenure is generally granted at the end of six years with your papers reviewed starting in the fall semester. For assistant professors, tenure is tied to promotion to associate professor. Rarely do universities grant tenure without promotion to associate professor.

Annual Faculty Review

Gaining tenure and promotion is based on the contributions of the new faculty member in three areas: teaching, service, and scholarship. Your performance in each of these three areas is reviewed by both the department's Personnel Committee (usually tenure-track faculty members elected by members of your department) and the Department Chair as outlined in departmental, college, and university guidelines for faculty and can generally be accessed from the Provost Office website. The annual review may take place to cover the January–December period or be based on the academic year, August–July. Also, each year you will be asked to submit a brief file (five to ten pages along with copies of articles/grants/presentations) representative of your professional accomplishments and achievements as well as your self-reflection and goals for the future. You will receive a letter signed by the Department Chair and Chair of the Personnel Committee (or even all members of the Personnel Committee) with comments. Upon receiving the letter, you may request to meet with the Department Chair and the Personnel Committee to get clarification or to challenge the results.

Teaching

Teaching includes courses you develop, courses you modify to improve the instruction and delivery to students, use of technology in your teaching, student evaluations, and master's and doctoral students you advise and mentor. Your syllabi will need to follow the department requirements in terms of course title, number, objectives, and, to a large degree, assignments as outlined by the department. You may have grading rubrics that all faculty teaching the course use. These are generally shared with students on the first day of class along with the syllabus, usually via the university's electronic computer course board such as Blackboard.

As a first-year faculty member, you'll likely be given a course release, sometimes two courses, to provide time for teaching preparation and research. Moreover, you may be given a graduate assistant to help out, particularly during the first year or if you are teaching large, entry-level classes. Keep in mind that when grades are given at the end of the semester, you, not the graduate or teaching assistant, will be held accountable. Likewise, if you rely heavily on your graduate or teaching assistant to cover your classes during much of the semester, the course evaluations by the students in the class may not be favorable.

If you have never taught a college-level course before, your skills—and likely patience as well—will be tested. Most universities have sessions for new faculty to learn instructional strategies and ways to assess students. Below are 17 proven tips to assist you in the classroom.

1. **Have a clear, organized syllabus that is available to students the first day of class—and stick to it.** Usually you will be provided with a sample master syllabus from another faculty member who has recently taught the course. This syllabus most likely would have been approved by the program. The syllabus must be followed for consistency and for accreditation purposes. Generally speaking, a faculty member can add to but not delete from a syllabus. For instance, one new faculty member thought the course title sounded outdated and changed it on her syllabus. She had created a nonexistent class causing her students anguish later on. Course titles are approved through a curricular process within the college and or department. Each course

in a department should have a unique set of objectives and requirements.

Most departments will provide photocopies of your syllabus provided you get the syllabus to the secretary at least three workdays before your class meets. Many universities post the syllabus on a department website and/or Blackboard or a university electronic equivalent. Some institutions require faculty to email syllabi to students to save the expense of printing.

Sometimes a list of approved textbooks for the course has been created by faculty. Under the term "academic freedom" you may select a recommended textbook but also other readings for the course as long as students read the recommended textbook(s) from the department. Select the textbook(s) and notify the bookstore of your selection at least a month prior to the beginning of the semester. These textbooks should be the ones that the program has indicated on the course syllabus you receive. You should also check with the department on how textbooks should be ordered. You may not be expected to order your own if there is a secretary or someone who is in charge of ordering all the textbooks. Generally if you contact the publisher, they will send you a free desk copy.

2. **In your syllabus, indicate specific expectations as to course requirements.** Give the specifications and due dates for all assignments. Then routinely give reminders in class of what assignment is coming up the following week. Include any rubrics for assignments with the syllabus. Likewise include a statement regarding cheating and plagiarizing and what course of action will be taken—an unfortunately common problem today, with the national media reporting that Harvard University, the Naval Academy, Florida State University, among others having large numbers of students cheating on online projects, term papers, and/or exams.

Indicate if late assignments are accepted and when the final cutoff is (i.e., a week later with one letter grade lowered). If you accept late papers, you may want to indicate that a late paper will be penalized. For instance, an assignment turned in the by next class session would be penalized 10%. Any assignment turned in over a week late may be given 50%. If quizzes or tests are given, you may opt to let students take makeup tests if they can provide medical statement from a doctor or the university health center or if they have a death in the family (for which they must provide a memorial card from the memorial service or funeral home). Other reasons are usually not accepted.

Some departments have policies about absences—so check. A rule of thumb is one absence per hour of course so three absences would be acceptable for a three-hour course, four for a four-hour course. It is a good idea to check with the program on the policies for absences, acceptance of late work, and points lost for late work so there is consistency. Students are always comparing professors who are teaching the same course under another section number and can easily call "not fair" if they feel other students are getting easier treatment than they are, which, in the long run, will be reflected in your student evaluations at the end of the semester. Likewise, students at some institutions will demand more rigor in their courses if they believe it is necessary to get a good job.

Also indicate that texting in class isn't acceptable behavior nor is being late to class. If you have a portion of the grade (usually 10%) devoted to attendance and participation, you can penalize students for such distracting behavior. It is best to take care of these issues, not only for your benefit but for the benefit of the entire class. Students do complain about their peers and are annoyed if the shortfalls are not addressed by the professor.

Include the university or department policy statement regarding assistance for students with special needs (hearing or vision loss, learning disabilities, etc.) and where on campus they can receive assistance. Likewise include a statement regarding cheating and plagiarizing and what course of action will be taken.

3. **On the first day of classes, give an assignment that is due on the second day of class.** It may only be a one-page paper or a two-page summary of a ten-page article students get online, or it may be the completion of three math problems, but the assignment demonstrates that you have high expectations of your students to get things done on time. It also provides an

opportunity for you to get a measure of the quality of their work early in the semester.

4. **Likewise, return graded assignments at the next class session or not later than one week later.** By so doing you will model responsible behavior. Students appreciate such effort on the instructor's part and most likely will give you favorable ratings on the course instructor's evaluation at the end of the semester. If you have a very large class, you may want to tell the students that just from a practical standpoint, it may take longer to grade their assignments. If for personal reasons (i.e., illness, or death in the family or other reasons that are not avoidable), always explain in advance that you will be doing your best to get their graded work back to them as soon as possible due to the circumstances. If you appear sincere and have worked well with them all semester, they will accept what you have to say.

5. **If you have thirty-five students or fewer in the class, get to know your students by their first names by the end of the second week of classes.** This helps you keep track of the students, and in turn, your students will feel that you value them as individuals. To assist with learning their names, take digital photos (if students give permission) (note that some universities include the student's photo along with name, university identification, and email address on the class list for the course section), make a seating chart, or cut file folders to make name placards that you hand out and collect at each class session. Also during each class session say each student's name at least twice (taking roll, returning assignments, putting them in groups, etc.). When you call on students, have them say their name before they contribute to the discussion. You aren't the only one learning the names of students as these tactics help their classmates as well. Depending on how many students you have and considering the practicality of this idea, you may want to have one-on-one office visits with each student for about fifteen minutes toward the beginning of the semester. This will allow you to know their strengths and weaknesses or find out things about them that will help you understand them better. When noticing a strength in terms of experience, you may want to ask them if they feel

Jerome Library, Bowling Green State University, Bowling Green, Ohio.

comfortable sharing their experiences with the class when the situation arises (e.g., an education major may have attended a charter school or a Montessori School and the individual's experience might provide a practical application to a topic discussed in class). A science major may have spent summers at Johns Hopkins University as a middle school student in their gifted education program. Another student may have grown up in an urban area and may have had experiences that other students may not have had, or a student may be here from another country and can share his/her culture's beliefs with others in the class. In some ways, these students are experts whose experiences bring new perspectives and practical experiences into your classroom. Students usually feel important and very honored to be considered an "expert" or at least a strong contributor.

6. **Model for your students so they learn how they can be organized for your class.** Include in the syllabus a one- or two-page outline of the readings and assignment due dates.

You might walk them through a Blackboard or electronic media session. Remind students in class of upcoming due dates for uploading papers or taking online exams. Have color-coordinated folders for different projects due during the semester or for in class group work. If your work requires a lot of library time, have a librarian come to your class and give a 30-minute demonstration or even meet in the library for an orientation. Explain rules for using a laboratory. Present the expectations for use of the Internet for the course as well as the use of smart phones, for example, as calculators or information locators.

7. **If you give an essay test, ask a student who received full credit for his/her answer for permission to read it to the class.** By noting on your test answer key the students who had the best responses and having those individuals read their answers aloud, other students can note what their own responses lacked. So you've turned this into learning situation for them. It also cuts down on complaints by students that you are grading unfairly or you just do not like them for some reason. If the test is online, you may discover students using the exact, word-for-word response for their essay. This is viewed as cheating and needs to be presented to the university student ethics board.

8. **Present grades in a fair manner.** Keep in mind undergraduates in many cases don't read the text before they come to class. They do the assignments the night before they are due. Some may only show up on the days when there are quizzes or tests if the class doesn't have an attendance requirement. Somehow you must figure out how to modify the typical college student's behavior so he/she will be on task and get the work accomplished for your course.

   If you use a point system for grading, making the more points possible a high number results in less anxiety for the students. For instance, if you have the same requirements for the course but use a 1,000-point total as opposed to a 100-point total, even if the percentages are the same, students will be more comfortable and less likely to question their grades on individual assignments and exams.

9. **Get to class early and stay a few minutes afterward; then go to your office and stay at least fifteen minutes.** This allows students to catch you and ask any questions they may have. You may want to periodically remind them of this practice you have set up for you and for them. It could slip their mind, so reminding them can help throughout the semester.

10. **Keep set office hours.** Usually it is better to be in your office an hour before your class meets and fifteen minutes after the class is over. This is a buffer for the students who may try to call you indicating they are sick and won't be in class. If you can't be there during your office hours for any reason, call the department secretary and have a note put on your office door. You can also have students email you, and you should be sure to check your email prior to going to class so you will know of any issues in advance. Texting students means they have your cell phone number and you theirs. It's better to keep it more remote, although there are ways to text students without giving them your own cell phone number.

    Make it clear that you are available to meet with students individually outside of class to go over projects, assignments, test results, whatever—but only in your office or lab—never off-campus or even in a public place. When you do meet with a student, keep your office door open. If you expect a confrontation, let a colleague in a nearby office know so that individual will be in his/her office—with the door open—to verify what took place in the meeting.

    And if you think the student may be unstable and in need of counseling, IMMEDIATELY alert your Department Chair or Assistant Chair. Write down any unusual behavior, times and dates, along with location, and keep a log on that student. This might include a female student repeatedly making appointments to see a young male or female faculty member for attention. Or a student who talks out loud to himself in class—seemingly unaware of what is taking place in class. Or a student who threatens you. Be certain you have the campus police phone number on your contact list for your cell phone.

11. **Make sure students know their bounds.** Students should not act inappropriately or have unreasonable expectations. Increasingly students tend to email your campus email address outside of reasonable hours—for instance at 2:00 AM with questions on an assignment due at 9:00 AM the same day despite your having gone over the details of the same assignment twice over the past three weeks in class.

    One student complained that a faculty member took too long to post results for tests when the faculty member walked across campus immediately after class to the testing center, which scanned the results while he waited and immediately posted them to the course electronic website—roughly twenty minutes after the last student turned in her exam scantron bubble form. This is a "want it right now generation."

12. **Provide students with advance notice if you are going to be out of town.** Nothing infuriates students more than getting out of bed for an 8:00 AM class that the instructor forgot to cancel before leaving for a conference. It is also helpful to explain to your students that it is expected that a professor attend conferences and present papers at these conferences for their own tenure/promotion as well as the fact that they must remain current of what is out in the field, so students won't look at your absence as an excuse to get away.

13. **Keep up with the technology students use.** If you typically send emails to let students know what they are to do for your class, be aware that undergraduates consider email an ancient form of communication, so you need to tell them to monitor their emails. Make sure your students realize the best way to communicate with you (i.e., email, Blackboard, or another course delivery platform). Remind them it is their responsibility to check all the places you may be trying to relay a message to the class. You will be counting on them to do that, and they need to know it is their responsibility. Undergraduates are more apt to text and tweet and may only occasionally check their email. Remind them that this will put them behind. It is not likely that a professor would use Twitter or Facebook

to communicate with the students. The academic side of technology is the way to go rather than the social networking side. On social networking they may learn more about you than they need to know and vice versa, so avoiding it is the best approach.

14. **Maintain confidentiality regarding information about students.** When returning papers and tests, fold them so other students can't see the grade or put the grade on the last page (a bit inconvenient for you, however, when you record the grades). Don't talk about students' grades or share personal information with other faculty. However, you may discuss a student in private with the student's advisor. Or you may mention to another faculty member who has the same student that the student has been frequently absent or seems distracted. If there is a pattern, the student may have issues outside of class that are interfering with his/her performance. You are hired to teach students, which means sometimes you need to go the extra mile to assist them in their learning.

15. **Be confident and don't waffle.** Be frank and honest with students. If students discover you are new, marginal students in particular are likely to try to manipulate you into either reducing course requirements or giving them higher grades. One student, for instance, began lobbying for an A from the midterm on. She had never had an A in the class but even after the semester was over continued to harass the faculty member to give her a higher grade or extra work to allow her to get a higher grade. The faculty member informed the student the standard was 92% for an A for the course and she had not met it and to give her additional assignments would be unfair to her classmates. The student finally acknowledged that she was a B student and needed the A. Instead of taking sole responsibility for delivering information students find distasteful, indicate to your classes that you are following program rules and your Department Chair is looking at you to do the right thing just as you are looking at the students to do the right thing.

16. **Exhibit a sincere passion about your subject matter.** You are obviously willing to devote your career to the study of and

teaching about your subject matter. Students should see you convey your devotion and enthusiasm during each and every class session.

17. **Keep tweaking your course material toward becoming efficient with your time and instruction.** Do not continuously lecture. Demonstrating and modeling help students retain and comprehend the material. For instance, walk the students through an activity. Research supports using a number of learning modalities also increases retention, such as showing an illustration, chart, diagram, or photogram on a document camera while you explain a concept. The students are processing aural *and* visual information, which can increase retention from 25% for just aural information (such as a lecture) to between 50 and 80% (Farris and Werderich, 2011).

Providing the key points of your lectures on PowerPoint slides via Blackboard or the university-based electronic learning system can assist students. However, some faculty believe having students take their own notes on lectures and class discussions helps them to better understand concepts being discussed as they put the information down in their own words. Moreover, some students feel that they can easily devote class time to their Facebook and texting activities with friends. Therefore, they participate less when they know that if they don't listen in class or don't attend class, they can still get the information electronically. Remember, though, to avoid lecturing directly from the PowerPoints and from what they have already read in the textbook. If you do this, and if students write down what you tell them, the information becomes redundant. You also run the risk of students becoming note-takers without processing the information. By keeping the PowerPoints brief and adding comments orally to enhance them, students will stay more alert and be more apt to attend classes, as they know they can't earn a good grade without attending class.

When you are in class with your students or even in informal conversation, it is best to remember that giving any indication that you are better than your colleagues is very inappropriate. When they complain about one of your colleagues to you, it is best not to roll your eyes or say that you already knew this about the person. Use this opportunity to explain professionalism to your students. This will also help them in their own future career. If students come to your office to complain about a colleague, share that they need to make an appointment with the Department Chair or Assistant Chair to air their concerns.

Many institutions allow student evaluations of instructors to weigh heavily. If you follow the guidelines presented above, you should be on the road to receiving high evaluations from your students. Nevertheless, students can and do go to administrators to say when they are unhappy. If it is necessary to meet with your Department Chair regarding a student complaint or an unfavorable evaluation, you want to be upfront, honest, and organized in the meeting. It is very uncomfortable to get an email from your Chairperson saying, "Can we talk? A large group of students just came to my office to complain about you." This is particularly awkward for the administrator, but the administrator must also keep in mind that the new faculty member finds this experience awkward and embarrassing. An administrator who chooses his/her words carefully and offers to help is a much more productive reaction than saying, "You need to shape up." Also some students routinely complain to the Department Chair if they think they are going to receive a low grade. One student never took notes and sat off by herself, feet propped up on the seat in front of her. When she got a "D" on the midterm, she went to the Department Chair and complained. On most campuses, the policy is for the student to first meet with the faculty member. However, in this case the Department Chair took the student's side. Fortunately, the new faculty member passed out the exams and collected them after going over the test with the class. He was able to show his Department Chair that the student had the lowest test score and missed items that 90% of the class answered correctly.

The administrator might assign a faculty mentor, specifically for teaching, to the new faculty member, a good problem-solving approach that is nonthreatening, productive, and won't be viewed as punitive. As a way to retain more students, universities have instructional resource centers where new faculty work with a faculty member with expertise in teaching practice who assist new faculty in honing their instructional skills.

Service

Service includes committees at the university (department, college, and university-wide) and involvement in your professional organizations. Service is needed to get tenure and promotion, but unlike teaching and scholarship, an overabundance of committee work is seldom given its due by the department and college committees that give their approval for tenure and promotion. It takes a tremendous amount of committee work for a department to function. Faculty serve on curriculum, personnel, and student committees at the department, college, and university levels. Faculty governance and graduate school committees tend to be demanding on a faculty member's time. Likewise, personnel committees are extremely time intensive as they review tenure and promotion as well as annual faculty performance reviews.

Before committing to serving on a committee make certain the task is given value. For instance, almost every institution requires department, college, and university service—at each level—in order to get tenure. There is a ranking of committees; however, it is generally not usually spelled out within a department, which can be somewhat frustrating. Generally speaking, committees that meet monthly outweigh those that meet once a semester. So Curriculum, Personnel, and the like outweigh Election, Library, and Homecoming Committees. Most departments elect people to serve on committees. Some departments rotate committee assignments, thereby giving everyone an opportunity to serve. Extra activities, such as working on parents weekend, may not count but be still be encouraged by the Department Chair. Attending commencement ceremonies may count as department service in one department but not in another at the same university.

Service in professional organizations may begin with volunteering to serve on a committee such as a Program Committee as a reviewer of papers submitted for presentations and later moving up to an elected position such as an officer. National organizations outweigh state or regional organizations. Service in professional organizations is one way that your institution gets notoriety in the field and as such is viewed as important by your department and college as well as your university. It is important that you offer your willingness to serve on committees to establish your name in your field.

At the end of each year of service on a committee it is a good idea to ask the committee Chair to write a letter detailing your service on that committee. Did you regularly attend meetings, take on additional tasks, and so forth? Save these letters for your personnel file for tenure and promotion. Some departments may ask that they be included in the annual personnel review.

Scholarship

Scholarship includes scholarly publications and presentations along with grant proposal writing. Your prime base to continue your scholarship is your doctoral dissertation from which you should yield at least one scholarly (peer reviewed, also known as refereed) article or a book chapter—perhaps even a book—and one professional presentation. Articles in peer reviewed and research journals tend to outweigh those in nonpeer reviewed publications. However, the number of issues of the publication and its rejection rate should be noted and recorded in your annual faculty review materials. You may look up this information in the Cabell Directory or email the editor of the journal. A book chapter is rated equal to or even higher than a refereed article. A book is generally rated the highest but only counts when it comes out in print. However, some institutions rate refereed, peer reviewed articles, book chapters, and books as being equally weighed.

Articles, book chapters, and books that have been referenced by others in their published works receive additional respect by your peers. You may check to see if your work is cited by others by going to Google Scholar and typing in your full name. National and international journals outweigh regional or state journals. Some universities have an index of rankings of publications, which is factored into the annual review process. Someone who continuously publishes in high-level journals will be noted in the field and likely to receive recognition within the college and university for his/her work.

Generally the deadline to submit a presentation proposal is six to eleven months before the conference. The components of the proposal will include the title of presentation or paper to be read, objectives, and an overview of the significance of the presentation with references to current theories and research. Sole presentations and papers may carry more weight than co-presentations. However, all are counted. National presentations are more highly regarded than regional or state presentations.

Grants are usually offered to new faculty by the college itself as a way to mentor new scholars. Almost every institution has grant-writing training sessions, with many offering a small stipend to those who attend. The office of the Associate Provost for Research will offer grant writing and budgeting assistance to all faculty and always encourages new faculty to pursue grants in their respective fields.

Writing articles, book chapters, books, or grants with colleagues can be helpful. That said, writing with colleagues can sometimes be difficult. It may not be easy to decide who is to be the lead author of a book or article or the principal investigator of the grant. A coauthor who never meets the deadlines you've agreed upon is a hurdle to a good relationship. If you opt to write with a senior professor who always insists upon having top billing, regardless of the amount of effort he/she has contributed to the project, you are placed in a very uncomfortable position. Writing with one colleague may go smoother than trying to write with three. Nevertheless, before agreeing to work on a project with someone else, find out if you have compatible work habits.

Other issues to keep in mind when deciding to work with someone else, if the faculty member doesn't have a track record, you cannot be certain if the person writes well, takes responsibility for the tasks assigned to him/her in a timely manner, is well respected by peers, and so forth. If the faculty member doesn't want to work evenings or weekends, that could be an obstacle in meeting a deadline. Being first author may carry more weight than serving as a secondary author.

Most larger institutions have writing groups of senior and junior faculty who review one another's manuscripts, giving critical comments before the junior faculty member submits to the journal or for a chapter in a book. When the institution is small, the writing group may be across disciplines. Such writing groups are helpful as they offer constructive criticism as well as provide deadlines for your writing. For instance, you may be expected to submit a manuscript each semester for the others to read—a nice schedule. Google docs or Dropbox are means of sharing manuscripts with other colleagues.

In times of tight funding, any faculty member who can write a grant that is subsequently funded has an advantage in gaining tenure and promotion. Submitting a number of grant proposals that aren't funded, however, may not be viewed favorably by some universities. Federally funded grants are rated higher than are state-funded grants. Certain foundation grants are considered to be "plums" in particular fields. Fulbright Awards are prized at all institutions.

Research papers submitted blindly and reviewed by peers provide a means for the university to gain attention in the field of study. A lack of travel funds hinders the faculty member from presenting at several conferences, as most universities will fund fully only one or two conference presentations. Be selective and stick to one or two professional organizations to present at and be involved as a member serving on committees or, better yet, as an officer. As such, you'll likely be able to submit proposals that will ultimately be accepted.

For those in the arts, the tenure/promotion process is similar in terms of teaching and service but not necessarily in terms of scholarship. Artists may have their works presented in blind judging events throughout the country or world. Musicians can have recitals at other universities, which count toward their scholarship activities. It is important to find out how such presentations or performances are viewed both within your department and within your college.

It is critical for the new faculty member to keep documentation and artifacts to demonstrate effectiveness and growth as a scholar. For example, the number of article submissions and subsequent publications and papers read at professional meetings should be balanced during the years leading up to tenure. A lack of articles, grant submissions, and presentations during the first three or four years followed by a flurry of article and paper submissions is sometimes referred to as the "tenure push" and gives the impression that the faculty member is inconsistent over time and might not make much of an attempt to obtain grants, conduct research, write scholarly articles, and present. Thus, granting tenure may become questionable.

It is critical that you be as accurate as possible when communicating the magnitude of your contribution to a project, such as a coauthored article, the presentation of a paper at a conference, or a grant award. List your name in the order it appears in the journal—not as first author unless you were the primary or lead author of the piece. If you were employed by a grant, indicate that so the reviewers can distinguish whether you were the principal author of the grant. Remember, the information can be checked by the committee and inaccuracies may put the candidate—you—in a negative light.

The Rating System for Annual Faculty Review

The key to getting tenure and promotion to associate professor is to get good ratings in each of the three areas—teaching, service, and scholarship—starting in your first year. While it is not uncommon for most new faculty to have one area that is weaker than the other two, any *significant* weaknesses may be cause for alarm—no research agenda or service on committees sends up a red flag. Likewise, no Department Chair wants to encounter a group of students who complain about the teaching of a new faculty member.

Most institutions will have a rating system that is outlined in the faculty personnel handbook. It may be a ten-point scale, a five-point scale, an unsatisfactory-satisfactory-exceptional spectrum, or other rating scheme. The differentiation between rankings must be spelled out in the faculty personnel guidelines for the department, college, and university. The department will have its own guidelines that meet the overarching personnel requirements of the college and university.

The rating system is applied separately for teaching, scholarly productivity, and service. Hence a faculty member may receive a low ranking for teaching but perhaps average for service and high in scholarly productivity.

Some institutions view teaching at the undergraduate level as being less important than teaching graduate-level courses. In rare circumstances, other institutions view it the opposite way, saying undergraduates are more demanding as they are novice learners in the field. Some colleges include advising students and serving on Doctoral and Thesis Committees as teaching while others list these under service to the department. The expectations concerning student advisement need to be clear as to the importance given to number of students advised, and Thesis and Doctoral Committees chaired or served on as a committee member.

Service is generally ranked as department committee work being of lesser value than college committee work, which holds lesser value than university committee work. Chairing a department or a college or university committee is given more weight than service as a committee member on the same committee.

Scholarship includes papers presented at professional conferences, publications (articles, book chapters, and books), and any recitals or exhibits with juried reviews. Peer reviewed papers for presentations and refereed journal articles are expected by most institutions. For scholarly productivity, typically departments may rank the levels of publications in terms of rigor and rejection rates. Other departments may actually rank journals from high to low in terms of degree of prestige in the field. Almost always refereed, peer-reviewed journals outweigh nonrefereed journals or newsletters. The exceptions are rare. In some fields, book chapters and books are given more prestige than refereed articles, while other fields give them weight equal to refereed articles.

A good dissertation Chair should have nurtured you to submit papers to professional organizations and submit refereed manuscripts to journals in your field, perhaps even serving as a co-presenter and coauthor with you. State and regional presentations demonstrate that you are beginning to become known in your profession. Even small grant submissions—including those not funded—are indicative that you plan to seek out funds for your research.

The Faculty Mentor

Generally you'll be assigned a faculty mentor from your department to help guide you through the annual review as well as the tenure and promotion process. The Department Chair, often in consultation with the Department Personnel Committee, makes this assignment, usually taking into consideration that the mentor would be a senior faculty member with strengths in teaching, service, and scholarship. You may or may not have input into this process. Sometimes an individual from the Search Committee will volunteer to serve as your mentor.

Early in your first semester—during the week of meetings before classes begin—you'll meet with your mentor to discuss your courses and the master syllabi from the department for each. You may set up a time to meet monthly throughout the first year, perhaps at a coffee shop or for lunch, to discuss your progress.

A good mentor will help you settle in with your classes first, and then suggest ways to meet the scholarship and service requirements, often suggesting journals for which your dissertation topic might be appealing for an article, or committees junior faculty typically serve on as members. The mentor may help you to be assigned to Thesis or Doctoral Committees.

Remember that the mentor was selected by the Department Chair and most likely is reporting back to that individual. Before you share too much information, consider how your Department Chair might interpret it. Stan seemed to be the perfect mentor for Christopher. Both had doctorates from Ivy League schools and loved their monthly lunches that stretched out for hours discussing topics in their field. Christopher mentioned to Stan an incident, which he considered to be minor, that occurred in his freshman class. The next week Christopher was called on the carpet by his Department Chair demanding to know what happened.

Stay or Venture to Greener Pastures?

By the end of the first semester, you have determined the lay of the land in your department. Your Department Chair has undoubtedly taken you to lunch. You've had meetings with a mentor faculty member. You've had your first course evaluations, and you've gotten the results early in the spring semester. And you may have submitted your first annual faculty report of your scholarship, teaching, and service. By the end of your first year or possibly sooner, you've decided whether or not you wish to stay to apply for tenure and promotion.

Even if you've decided to stay, you may have been checking your professional organization's listserve for job listings or *The Chronicle of Higher Education* to see if an enticing dream position has been posted. Be careful who you let in on your meanderings about leaving, because the department spent a lot of money for the search, which ended with your employment. Also the department would be without a tenure-track faculty member of your expertise for a year, usually until the new faculty member would be hired.

Roles of Administrators

The Department Chair and Dean of the College need to keep new hires happy but not to the detriment of current tenure-track faculty. Challenging fiscal times makes this even more complicated as often new hires come in at higher salaries than those hired only a few years earlier due to what is called "stagflation." It isn't unusual for a new hire assistant professor to come in at a salary more than a newly promoted associate professor. Obviously the associate professor with the superior vita in terms of scholarship and service isn't going to be pleased with the situation.

Keeping faculty happy can also mean providing research and travel assistance. A Dean or Department Chair who administers fairly is usually respected and often beloved by faculty and staff whereas those who give favors to friends or a particular area within a college or department usually end up in trouble. Consider the Dean who was promoted from within his own college. As a favor to members of his former department, he used his Dean's budget to cover all their travel costs to conferences—even a couple in Europe. Faculty in other departments were resentful, and eventually the Dean was limited to a single term of six years in the position.

The Department Chair usually takes each new faculty member to lunch or dinner for a one on one conversation during both the spring and fall semesters. In addition, first- and second-year faculty may be invited to a lunch with the Department Chair to exchange concerns or answer questions that may arise. In a small college the Dean may also have a luncheon for new faculty each year.

New faculty may find that the match isn't what they expected and may ask the Chair for a letter of recommendation so they may move along. Sometimes this can put the Chair in a difficult position. It is wise to have the university legal counsel review any letter of recommendation for a faculty member who has not measured up to expectations so a lawsuit might not be filed against the institution should the person fail to get another position.

If a faculty member has performed extremely poorly or behaved in unprofessional manner that has been documented (e.g., the faculty member repeatedly failed to grade assignments or exams, failed to return email and phone messages of students, made sexual advances toward students, came to class intoxicated), then the individual can be terminated as per the personnel guidelines of the institution. Becoming increasingly a concern is the lack of collegiality demonstrated by a new faculty member. A disruptive faculty member can make a Department Chair's life miserable as well as many faculty and staff members within a department. New faculty members who have temper tantrums, are disrespectful to peers and students, or who are overly demanding may best be encouraged to move on to another institution.

EPILOGUE

The new institution will welcome energetic faculty who have new ideas. It is up to the new faculty member to carve out a niche in research and teaching that both satisfies himself/herself and meets the relative needs of the department and the college at large.

Scenario One: The Wrong Fit

Marcia thought she'd love a large public university with lots of colleagues to share ideas and theories. Her interview had gone well and she seemed to get a sense of comradery. While she spent several hours in the lab to which she was assigned, she was surrounded with graduate students— not her peers. During the second department meeting of the semester, two male faculty members came to blows over a dispute over lab space. By the end of the semester it was clear there were several factions in the department. Life was unpleasant in Marcia's world, so she decided to go to a smaller institution with a higher course load and fewer notable researchers but where the faculty welcomed and supported her work.

Scenario Two: To Put Down Roots or Not

James and Natalie were both new faculty members in a department. James bought a house in the community upon his arrival while Natalie rented an apartment. James told Natalie that the faculty would see that he was interested in continuing his career at the college because of his purchase of a home there. Natalie informed James that she thought he had made a mistake, because if he didn't like the college, he'd want to leave and have to sell the house. He'd likely lose money on the house. By renting, she told him, the faculty would think they needed her and would try to entice her to stay by providing her additional opportunities and support, such as giving her graduate assistants, stipends for extra committee work, and the like.

Scenario Three: Finding the Perfect Fit

Mason loved his new university—a perfect fit!!! However, his wife was miserable. She was from the South and disliked the cold winters in Pennsylvania. Although his salary was rather high for a beginning assistant professor in his field and their children were in excellent schools, she insisted that Mason look for a position in a warmer climate. Mason found a position near where he had gotten his doctorate, and they moved after his second year at University A. However, the new position had a lower salary and less support for research and travel than his first position.

Scenario Four: Becoming Too Friendly with Students

Ted was an up-and-coming researcher who was adored by his colleagues and students. Every Friday at lunch, Ted and a few other faculty members and research assistants would head to a nearby pub. But while others left after an hour or two, Ted and some research assistants stayed and drank until late afternoon. Word got back to the Department Chair who backed Ted as she felt that he was a promising researcher. Eventually a research assistant complained about Ted's behavior and filed a complaint against him. Then another came forth. Finally Ted was told he would have to change his behavior if he wished to stay at the institution.

Scenario Five: Avoiding a Collision Course with Colleagues

Deborah was a talented researcher, and both undergraduate and graduate students loved her. However, she felt her skills were superior to those of a more senior faculty member who taught a graduate course that Deborah coveted. Since the course was offered only once a year, Deborah knew she would have to wait for several years before she could teach it—likely after her colleague retired. However, Deborah went to lunch with the more senior colleague and they discussed the course. The senior colleague was open to taking turns teaching the course. Deborah was pleased with the opportunity. Rather than going to the Department Chair, which the more senior colleague might have misconstrued as going behind her back, the open conversation about the course proved to be a successful way to open the door for Deborah.

Opposite page: Dance Building, University of Arizona, Tucson.

4

Gaining Tenure
and Promotion

Mid-career years translate to your continual work toward tenure and promotion to associate professor and growth to become a nationally recognized scholar in your field. Before that occurs, most institutions do a third-year review that takes place in the fall of the third year. Then, hopefully, it's onward and upward to full professor—the greatest job on earth. Each year you must work on improving your teaching, service, and scholarship. And it is extremely difficult to juggle all three—but it's necessary.

The Third-Year Review

After you've been at an institution for three years, you have the third-year review—which will be indicative of whether you will likely achieve tenure and promotion by your department. The third-year review is a compilation of your teaching, service, and scholarship, usually over the course of the first two years at your institution, which is presented in the fall of your third year. It likely was included in your annual review materials. The Department Chair and Personnel Committee (comprised usually of tenured faculty from your department) examine what you have accomplished during this period. Have your teaching evaluations by students improved? Are you serving on Master's Theses and Doctoral Committees? Are you serving on committees at all three levels (department, college, and university) as well as in your professional organizations? Are you presenting at professional meetings? Have you published in peer reviewed journals or had your work in juried reviews?

While you may feel you have done an adequate amount of representative work in each area, the Department Chair and Personnel Committee will ascertain whether your present level of contributions in each area suffices to gain tenure and promotion within the department. You may be compared to other faculty within the department. Should there be a superstar assistant professor who repeatedly gains grants or publishes in top research journals and you are only getting small grants and publishing in lesser known journals, the review may indicate that you need to stretch yourself to perform at a higher level.

The letter conveying the outcome of the third-year review generally is presented by the end of the first semester of year three, giving you adequate time to improve or to seek employment at another institution if your work fails to meet the department standards. Remember, tenure is granted by the department, not by the college or university. It is your peers and the Department Chair who are judging your professional work firsthand. While your tenure and promotion papers proceed to the college level—to the Dean and the College Personnel Committee—and even to the university level, should there be a negative decision at the department and/or college levels, it is largely the decision at the departmental level that weighs most heavily.

Should the third-year review be highly negative, the department may elect to terminate your employment. Usually this notification would be early in the second semester, effective at the end of the academic year or at the end of your fourth year at the institution. You may be permitted to appeal the findings at the departmental level, but the department decision is usually upheld unless there were most unusual circumstances (as tenure and promotion decisions reside in the department).

Tenure and Promotion

Tenure and promotion to associate professor is a major accomplishment for any faculty member and generally takes place after the sixth year. Tenure means that your employment is assured as long as you desire to work at that institution and your field offers a degree or is a service area to a degree area. Promotion means you are no longer a junior faculty member; furthermore it typically means a nice raise in your salary, usually ranging from $3,000 to $7,000 or more annually, although some institutions do not give a raise for promotions.

Colleges and universities rarely separate tenure from promotion to associate professor. The reasoning is that the faculty member has proven to be a good instructor, provide service to the university community, and consistently demonstrate scholarly productivity, so the university would support the promotion to associate professor and retaining the employee long term.

In order to keep on track for tenure and promotion, you must lay out a plan beginning in your first year at the institution to meet the expectations and then revisit it every six months to make certain you are on track. For instance, create a computer file for tenure and promotion, which charts your teaching and lists your courses and course evaluations, your master's advisees by year, your doctoral students' dissertations, and any innovations you have generated to enhance instruction in your courses. Create a paper file of student comments, cards, notes, and other relevant materials related to your students' feedback about your teaching. Create a second computer file to track all of your service activities, particularly noting whether you are serving/have served on department, college, and university committees as well as your involvement with professional organizations. Maintain a third file for scholarly productivity, including grant submissions, manuscripts submissions, and research projects. An Excel spreadsheet might be a good way to document and keep track of this type of information. Another way is to mount a bulletin board on your office wall. Below is an example of a bulletin board used by one of the authors to provide herself with a visual in her office of her scholarly productivity. As projects were completed or various stages advanced, color-coded index cards moved across the bulletin board (writing projects were yellow index cards; grants green; research blue).

The Tenure and Promotion Dossier

Going up for tenure and promotion will include collecting several documents and keeping them in a dossier. Below is a list of what most institutions expect:

- Request for tenure and promotion (usually a one page form from the university)
- Current curriculum vitae
- Annual reviews from the Department Personnel Committee and Department Chair
- Student course evaluations since you arrived on campus
- Collection of scholarly peer reviewed publications, papers read at professional conferences, and grant proposals, both funded and nonfunded

Scholarly Productivity Bulletin Board

Idea Stage	Coauthors/ Researchers	Draft One	Revision	Submission	Accepted	Published/ Journal or Presented

Each index card indicates the following:

- Date of initial idea
- Coauthors or researchers
- Date of first draft
- Date of revisions
- Date of submission (and to which journals on back of card so visitors to the office won't be able to read unless the card is taken off the board to read, thus any rejections are known only to you)
- Date of acceptance
- Date published

The Scholarly Productivity Bulletin Board aids in keeping you on task to move the index cards to the right for either publication in a refereed, peer reviewed journal or as a book chapter, or the presentation at a peer reviewed conference.

- Documentation of service on committees
- Other documentation regarding your professional teaching, service, and/or scholarly productivity

Most universities require that your dossier be comprehensive. Indeed some universities insist that faculty purchase plastic bins or tubs and in which they place file folders labeled for each artifact included in the dossier, complete with a table of contents at the front. Other institutions will just require a binder with the size specified in the university's faculty handbook. Again, the table of contents will need to be included in the binder.

Your curriculum vitae (CV) needs to accurately represent your professional history in terms of degrees obtained and years, work history, publications, presentations, and grants. Each institution has a prescribed order in which the CV needs to be placed and labeled.

Failure to follow university procedures can mean denial of tenure and promotion. Certainly have someone proofread your CV prior to submitting it to your department, usually early in the spring semester of your fifth year, as your CV and sample articles are generally sent out over the summer for review by senior faculty at comparable institutions. Normally members of the Department Personnel Committee along with the Department Chair will tag any typos for you to change before the CV and rest of the dossier are submitted to the college level. However, you don't really want your colleagues to be pointing out spelling and grammatical errors.

Outside Reviewers

As mentioned earlier, many colleges and universities send the CV along with a couple of writing samples to outside reviewers—faculty who are associate or full professors within your field at comparable institutions. Typically you may be asked to create a list of four or five potential outside reviewers who are individuals with whom you are not socially friends and have never coauthored professional publications or co-presented with at professional conferences. The Department Chair and Department Personnel Committee will come up with a similar list of outside reviewers. This list is generated in late spring or early summer before you submit your papers for tenure and promotion. The Department Chair and Department Personnel Committee then decide to whom they will send the materials to for review. Sometimes an outside reviewer isn't available or declines the offer, so the next person on the list is contacted. Normally there may be three outside reviewers selected from your list and three from the list generated by the Department Chair in discussions with the Department Personnel Committee.

Some universities give a modest honorarium of $50 to $100 to the outside reviewers. Others don't pay outside reviewers but send them a letter of appreciation for their professional expertise, which the reviewer can then use for his/her own service as part of his/her annual faculty review.

The outside reviewers are directed to evaluate your CV, which has accompanied your materials, in terms of teaching, service, and scholarly productivity as it relates to your department, college, and university guidelines. In addition, the outside reviewers read and critique your articles to judge in terms of contribution to your field of study as well as the rigor of the journal in which they were published (i.e., peer reviewed vs. nonpeer reviewed). Unless you specify the student course evaluations for all university courses taught or have been the recipient of teaching awards, most outside reviewers tend to indicate they cannot evaluate your teaching as they have no basis for such an evaluation. For service and scholarly productivity, the outside reviewers are comparing your committee work and publications, presentations, and grantsmanship with those expected at their own institution as well as with the guidelines of your institution.

Tenure and Promotion Review at Department, College, and University Levels

As mentioned earlier, the decision to grant tenure lies in the department. The majority of colleges and universities have the Department Chair and the Department Personnel Committee review the tenure/promotion candidate's materials in compliance with the faculty handbook and the expectations within the department, college, and university. Small liberal arts colleges generally weigh teaching more heavily than service or scholarship, while large research institutions give more weight to research activities. The outside reviewers' comments and results of each of the annual reviews along with the third-year review are also considered.

Typically there are separate opinions—the Department Chair's opinion and the Department Personnel Committee's opinion—as to whether tenure should be granted as well as promotion (separate votes on each). Each opinion is written in a letter addressing teaching, scholarship, and service that is sent along with the candidate's dossier to the Dean of the College and the College Personnel Committee. The process is then repeated there with the Dean and the College Personnel Committee each writing an opinion again on tenure and another opinion on promotion.

The Tenure and Promotion Decision

The decision for tenure and promotion is based to some degree on the steadiness and growth of the candidate. Is the teaching improving over the period in which the individual has been at the institution? Is the number of article publications increasing and have articles begun to appear in more rigorous journals? Is the number of grant submissions increasing and resulting in larger grant amounts than in the first years of the candidates employment? Does service cross department, college, and university lines as well as take place in a variety of professional organizations?

Should all the votes be in favor of both tenure and promotion, letters from the Department Chair, Department Personnel Committee, Dean, and College Personnel Committee are sent to the Provost's office for the final decision, which is almost always in agreement. Only in rare circumstances are tenure and promotion split with the assistant professor being recommended to be retained as an assistant professor with tenure without promotion to associate professor. Should there be a difference of opinion on granting tenure with promotion at the department level, the candidate has the right to appeal the decision by meeting with either the Department Chair, the Department Personnel Committee, or both. At most institutions, the candidate has the right to bring an advocate to the meeting to speak on the candidate's behalf. The turnaround for the reconsideration of the tenure/promotion review by the Department Chair and the Department Personnel Committee is usually very quick, sometimes within ten working days, so the candidate needs to act swiftly to address any concerns presented in the letters from both the Department Chair and the Department Personnel Committee. The same process may be repeated for a negative vote by either the Dean or the College Personnel Committee.

If the vote out of the department and college turns out to be in favor of denying tenure and/or promotion, the candidate may appeal at the university level before the Provost and the University Personnel Committee. Again an advocate may speak on the behalf of the candidate.

The rules for appealing tenure and promotion procedures are specified in the university, college, and department faculty handbooks, which are given to new faculty upon their arrival on campus. Usually these

Johnson Hall, University of Oregon, Eugene.

personnel guidelines are available online on the department, college, and university (Provost Office) websites. The personnel guidelines set at the university level cover all faculty. Each college and department may further refine the guidelines, but any differences must be approved at the department, college, and university levels. The personnel guidelines are reviewed periodically and dated with the last approved adoption.

Tenure and promotion cannot be denied due to sex, race or nationality, age (those over 40), religion (unless the school is private and has a religious affiliation), and disability status. Sexual preference cannot be a factor, but that depends on state law. Increasingly universities are adding a fourth consideration for tenure and promotion—collegiality of the candidate within the department. A disruptive faculty member can tank faculty morale across the department causing waves that the Department Chair must at times need to resolve.

Should the university decide to deny tenure, the university may elect to terminate the candidate at the end of the academic year. However, many colleges and universities provide for an additional academic year at the same salary as a measure of goodwill to assist the individual in transitioning to another position at another institution. Nevertheless, if the faculty member is unable to find a position, that is that faculty member's problem. Sometimes the university may have an instructor's position available at an instructor's pay rate and let the faculty member stay in that capacity. Generally, though, this is not the case.

In some instances a denial of tenure and promotion may end up in court. For decades, the court system refused to address tenure and promotion lawsuits, saying it was the decision of the institution. However, in the past thirty years, federal courts have ruled in some cases, particularly when an individual has been discriminated against in some way. The federal courts have also ruled that a tenure and promotion candidate may sue the Department Chair *and* individual members of the Department Personnel Committee in civil courts for damages resulting from denying tenure and promotion. Such cases typically drag out for months and years during which time the individual may not have a faculty position at the institution or at any other college or university in the United States, as word will get out about the legal issues via the Internet or social media.

Epilogue

Scenario One: Family and Medical Leave Act

Erin was delighted to learn that she was pregnant but concerned that the baby was due during the academic year. The tenure clock was ticking, and she was worried that being on maternity leave would hurt her chances for tenure. She made an appointment with her Chair who shared the Family and Medical Leave Act (FMLA), which is a federal law, with her. The federal guidelines permit a faculty member to take up to twelve weeks of leave if the individual is having or adopting a baby, needs to care for a family member, or has some medical issue in which he/she cannot work. During that period the faculty member continues to have health insurance and is paid based on the number of long-term care and sick-leave days he/she has accumulated. When Erin had her baby, she enjoyed staying home as a new mom, and her classes were covered by instructors until she returned.

Scenario Two: Publishing Outside of Your Field

Amanda's master's degree was in another field of business—marketing—than her doctorate—finance. She enjoyed researching in the area of marketing and continued to publish in the field in peer reviewed journals. When she submitted her dossier for tenure and promotion, she had only a couple of peer reviewed articles in the area of finance, which was both her field and her department. This was noted as an issue by a majority of the outside reviewers, including the ones she had selected. Upon making the final decision, her Department Chair—who was new—and the Department Personnel Committee declined to offer her tenure. The decision at the college level by both the Dean and the College Personnel Committee was in favor of giving her both tenure and promotion. Because the Department Chair and Department Personnel Committee differed from the Dean's and College Personnel Committee's decision, Amanda's tenure and promotion had to be appealed at the University Personnel Committee, which was chaired by the Provost. She appealed and subsequently gained tenure and promotion, as the University Personnel Committee and the Provost ruled that the department had not specified in the annual reviews that her scholarly publications were outside of her field.

Scenario Three: Presenting a Polished Dossier

Stanley was well liked in the department and seemingly on target for tenure and promotion. Upon submitting his tenure and promotion dossier, the Department Chair and Department Personnel Committee noticed numerous typos and grammatical errors. The Chair of the Department Personnel Committee was given the task of reviewing the dossier and providing Stanley with a list of the needed corrections and formatting to match the university requirements. Upon meeting with Stanley, the Chair of the Department Personnel Committee was told by Stanley that he "didn't have time for that kind of stuff," and he declined to edit his curriculum vitae for typos and errors. The Department Chair who had hired Stanley then emailed Stanley and got the same response. The Department Chair and the Department Personnel Committee then met to discuss the issue. To send the materials forward with numerous typos would reflect poorly on their department once they were reviewed by the Dean and the College Personnel Committee. The decision was made to have the department secretary make typo and grammatical corrections in order not to embarrass the department and then forward all the paperwork to the College Personnel Committee. Stanley was given tenure and promotion.

Scenario Four: Tenure and Promotion for a Rebellious Colleague

Linda was a great grant getter, typically bringing in a half million dollars a year for the department. Indeed, Linda was often the leading grant recipient in the department. However, Linda was impossible to work with. She made both her colleagues and members of the secretarial staff's lives miserable. She would post notes near the elevator to encourage students to enroll in her courses—and remove any such notes posted by her colleagues. During meetings she would sit near the center of the table and often slammed the table with her fist to make a point—much to the dismay of others. Linda used social media to promote herself, often making snide remarks about others in her department without naming them directly. She frequently refused to serve on committees, as she felt that it was a waste of her talents and time. In short, her peers viewed her as a bully. The Department Chair who had hired Linda retired, and the Dean appointed an Interim Chair for a year—the same year as Linda's promotion and tenure papers were reviewed. The Interim Chair carefully reviewed Linda's tenure and promotion criteria and dossier; then he voted against Linda's tenure and promotion. The Department Personnel Committee did likewise. The same results occurred at the college level with the Dean and the College Personnel Committee. Linda appealed at each level and took it across campus, appealing to the University Personnel Committee and the Provost, but the results were upheld at the department, college, and university levels. Because she was such a prolific grant writer, she was able to get a tenure-track position at another institution at the associate professor rank for the next academic year.

Scenario Five: A Cultural Difference

Hao was a native of Vietnam who spoke fairly good English. Her students, however, often expressed difficulty in understanding her. She spoke both quickly and softly, making it problematic for students in the back of the lecture hall to hear her even when she wore a microphone. Upon going up for tenure and promotion, Hao did not believe her language issue would be a problem as it had never been brought up during the annual reviews. However, both her Department Chair and the Department Personnel Committee cited her language issues as a major teaching deficiency and she was denied tenure and promotion at the private college. Because of her strong scholarship record, she was able to get a position at another institution.

Scenario Six: Different Standards for a Male versus a Female Faculty Member

Mark and Miranda were hired at the same time in the same department. Miranda had very strong teaching and scholarly publication records while Mark's were rather minimal. Their service records were about equal. Their Department Chair was a male who had a reputation for cheating on his wife with graduate students. He even called Miranda in the wee hours of a Saturday morning wanting her to meet him for a drink. When Mark and Miranda submitted their tenure and promotion dossiers it was apparent that Mark's work would be under scrutiny at the college level. The Department Chair informed Miranda that she needed to "refine her curriculum vitae" and take some things out. He even gave her a marked up version of her curriculum vitae. Miranda wasn't certain what to do. She didn't have a mentor within the department, so she went to the university's faculty advisor who advised that as long as everything within her CV was accurate, she should leave it as is. Miranda elected not to make any changes. The Department Chair then asked the Department Personnel Committee for recommendations to evaluate both Mark and Miranda. Since the Department Chair was responsible for sending out the CVs and sample articles, he selected individuals for Miranda's review who were the top-notch experts in the field of study while Mark's body of academic work was reviewed by faculty—none of whom held the rank of full professor and all whom were at lesser institutions. Both Mark and Miranda were granted tenure and promotion, but Miranda often wondered, if the criteria had been even, would Mark have gotten both tenure and promotion?

Scenario Seven: Competing When the Rules Change

Frank was hired at a university and given a three and three course schedule. The following year two more assistant professors were hired but given a two- and three-course load to teach. During the annual review process, Frank's work was always compared with the two newer faculty who had more time during one semester each year to conduct research and write up the findings for papers for professional presentations at conferences and chapters in books. Increasingly, Frank felt frustrated at being unable to keep up with the two new faculty. His annual reviews ranked his achievements lower than his peers. Frank met with his Department Chair who said he would be expected to meet the same criteria for tenure and promotion that was spelled out in the department, college, and university faculty handbooks. Frank subsequently gained tenure and promotion but felt he had been required to go an extra mile compared to his two junior colleagues.

Opposite page: West corner of Willamette Hall, University of Oregon, Eugene.

5

Midcareer Goals

Once you've achieved tenure and been promoted to associate professor, you may feel that you can relax and take it easy—hop off the "publish or perish" roller coaster and kick back a bit. Perhaps you are comfortable staying in rank as an associate professor. But promotion to full professor is the real brass ring in academia. Full professors make the higher salaries and tend to hold more weight in departmental and college discussions when important decisions are made. Driving onward to attain the rank of full professor may lead you to other avenues and open doors in your career.

More and more, universities are doing tenure-track reviews of long-term faculty. The long-term work is evaluated—such as every ten years—similarly to what a third-year review would be. The Department Personnel Committee and the Department Chair review the faculty member's teaching, service, and scholarly productivity to maintain academic quality in the department, and the faculty member is given a report indicating his/her strengths and weaknesses in each of these three areas. The report might include suggestions, such as use more technology in teaching, develop better rapport with students, become better organized in your class lectures, and so on; serve on more department, college, and university committees; pursue grants; or submit manuscripts to higher level refereed journals.

This chapter will examine long-term possibilities with regard to remaining as an associate professor, moving up to full professor, or becoming an administrator.

Staying as an Associate Professor

Some faculty elect to devote most of their careers to teaching and service, spending less time on research and scholarly engagement. They may be very comfortable remaining as associate professors and focus on the opportunity to become the leading instructors in their departments and colleges, to mentor new faculty in teaching and service, or to chair Curriculum Revision and Course Development Committees. Administrators may call on them to write accreditation reports because they know the curriculum inside and out.

Such individuals will still present papers at professional conferences and submit manuscripts for publication. They have to continue to present and submit and publish or the colleges or universities can terminate them, but they aren't on the rapid climb to become nationally recognized scholars. Dismissal for lack of presentations and publications, however, is so rare that it becomes newsworthy and front-page material. It is far more likely that a faculty member is dismissed for engaging in inappropriate conduct (e.g., plagiarism; submitting false travel vouchers; sexually harassing students, staff, or other faculty; being found guilty of a felony).

Getting Promoted to Full Professor

"Best job in the world! Full professor!" Bill loved to say, relishing being a full professor in the College of Business. And he was right in many aspects. Being a full professor means you have earned respect, your work is recognized as making contributions to the field, and you are a leader on campus. Likely when you present at conferences, people come up to you to discuss your research findings or an article you published. Sure, students can offer up a few headaches, and your Chair's can pressure you to go after yet another grant, but by and large, full professors live very well and are financially rewarded for their efforts. To check to see the differences in salary between the average assistant, associate, and full professors at your university, Google faculty salaries at universities and you'll see an option for Interactive Table: Average Salaries of Full-time Professors published each April in the *Chronicle of Higher Education* for public and private four-year colleges, and a number of community colleges. Salary at doctoral awarding universities is substantially higher than at four-year colleges without graduate programs. Remember that the figures presented are averages across disciplines, with the Sciences and Business departments typically paying far greater than the Arts, Humanities, and Social Sciences departments.

Full professors are most apt to serve as mentors to new assistant professors. The desire by a Department Chair to have a model faculty member for the new assistant professors to emulate means the full professor has demonstrated quality teaching, significant service leadership, and high productivity in research, presenting, and writing book chapters and books as well as articles for scholarly journals.

Full professors tend to hold responsible positions on committees and are elected as officers in state and national professional organizations within their fields of study. They may do research or consultant work outside the institution or for accreditation purposes for colleges and universities. They are approached by corporations and publishers who pay them for their expertise. They may be featured speakers at conferences, rewarded with nice honoraria for their speeches.

In short, a full professor has a great deal of flexibility in selecting what he/she wants to teach, topics for research, and committees on which to serve. Should the department get a new Chair who is not easy to get along with, the full professor can avoid confrontations by arranging office hours to meet student needs but not run into the Department Chair every few hours during the day.

Seeking an Administrative Position

Associate or full professors may want to seek an administrative position such as Assistant Chair or Department Chair, which involves working with colleagues within a department, or with the Assistant or Associate Dean, and removes the professor from the front line of working directly with students. Such positions may offer a reduced teaching load as well as an increased salary along with additional responsibilities. Being an Assistant Dean or Associate Dean isn't as difficult as serving as Department Chair who has to deal directly with problem faculty and staff and students with issues day after day. Additional duties include budgeting issues and trying to get donations from alumni and others to enhance the department.

Moving up from being a faculty member to running the entire department as Department Chair is a major step. Colleagues who once supported you as a peer now consider you as their boss. When annual evaluations are done, you must have an even hand and not play favorites. Having your own posse may make things seem easier for you, but it will lead to the likelihood that a group of faculty will someday conduct a coup on your leadership by going behind your back to the Dean to have you removed as Chair.

Positions such as Assistant or Associate Dean tend to have built-in buffer zones. While Department Chairs are in the trenches, with faculty seeing and critiquing nearly every decision the Chair makes, Assistant and Associate Deans serve at the pleasure of the Dean, and their work assignments are largely directed by the Dean. If an Assistant Dean is in charge of assessment within the college, that individual may not be cheered for gathering data, but faculty acknowledge that the work is essential for accreditation purposes.

While associate and full professors, and to some extent assistant professors, have control over how many hours they work each week, administrators generally work at least forty hours a week. Increasingly, university administrators are asked to spend a portion of their time assisting members of the school's foundation staff in securing donations from alumni and friends of the department and college. Such development work may be done during the evenings or on weekends and may require some travel to the locations where the potential donors reside.

Being an administrator requires knowledge of the legal rights of students, faculty, and staff. Serving as a Chair of a department, a position that is covered by a union contract with the school, necessitates understanding that contract or employment agreement.

Far too many faculty members believe they have the skill set to be a good Department Chair only to discover after they get into the position that they aren't suited for it. Department Chairs are responsible for creating a budgets, making personnel decisions that are in the best interest of the institution, maintaining an even temper, meeting deadlines, problem solving, among many other tasks that are not necessarily spelled out in the "job description." Thus, the inability to perform well in these areas can lead to a Chair's downfall. If you have trouble maintaining your cool, can't take criticism, get upset when deadlines aren't met by others, you may not want to be a Department Chair.

Some individuals play favorites once they've become an administrator—which only serves to divide faculty and lower morale. It is very difficult to be objective and fair when you've been selected by your peers to serve in a supervisory capacity.

Ullrich Hall, University of Wisconsin, Platteville.

Possible Consequences of Relocating to Another State

On occasion a colleague might email you about a lucrative position that has opened up at a "perfect" college in hopes you'll apply for the position. Indeed, in the 1960s it was commonplace for Deans to stay at universities and faculty to move from time to time. Now, however, the structure of pension and Social Security benefits as well as fewer senior faculty-level openings result in fewer moves by faculty. Thirteen states, for instance, require that state employees who are qualified to receive a state pension, such as faculty at public universities, receive reduced Social Security benefits of up to 40 percent depending on the number of years and amount of income they earned as part of a state pension program (this is referred to as the Windfall Elimination Provision (WEP). Thus, if a faculty member moves from a state in which Social Security is part of the pension package to a state that has a state pension plan for university faculty, that individual's Social Security benefits will be reduced as part of the WEP.

The WEP reduces the Social Security benefit for retired and disabled workers receiving pensions from non-Social Security covered employment. The WEP reduces the factor by which average earnings are multiplied to determine Social Security benefits. The amount of reduction depends on when the person retires and how many years of Social Security earnings he/she has accumulated. The reduction may be no more than one-half of the government pension to which the person is entitled in the initial month of entitlement to the pension. Some of the states with state pension plans include Alaska, California, Colorado, Connecticut, Georgia, Illinois, Kentucky, Louisiana, Maine, Massachusetts, Missouri, Nevada, Ohio, Rhode Island, and Texas (National Education Association, 2014).

If you are married and die before your spouse, your spouse might receive a reduction in spousal Social Security benefits if you have a public state pension and also qualify for Social Security. This is referred to as the Government Pension Offset.

Roles of Administrators

Some institutions offer internships either within the college or within university for faculty to test their desire to become administrators. Larger institutions hold training sessions to build leadership skills. Tasks that hold responsibility while letting the faculty member get a taste of administration are assigned. Such situations enhance leadership skills on campuses and help individual faculty determine whether he/she truly wants to serve in an administrative capacity and meet the rigorous demands of being an administrator.

Deans and Provosts can select faculty that they believe have strong leadership skills to chair ad hoc committees. Such leadership activities help develop the necessary skills to be a successful university administrator.

On occasion there are assistant professors who are introverts and who find teaching to be a painful experience or, at the least, something they do not enjoy. However, such faculty may have skills that the college needs, such as conducting self-studies of the institution for accreditation or state reports. Deans and other upper level administrators need to find ways to both assist such faculty in developing their instructional skills and pedagogy as well as offer alternatives to a traditional teaching/research/service model.

EPILOGUE

Scenario One: Being Forced to Become an Administrator

Susan was well organized, popular with graduate students, and recognized nationally for her research. While she served on several committees, she had avoided becoming an administrator. "Not my cup of tea," she'd respond when Deans would ask her to chair her department. Then her Chair left for a Dean's position at another institution. Most of the faculty within the department were either ready to retire or had been hired within the past two years. She was named Acting Chair for the year. Susan delved into the job. She was comfortable leading faculty meetings and making necessary decisions that pertained to the department. She wasn't fond of having to prod the faculty into making decisions regarding modifications in the personnel process as part of a university-wide plan. When it came time for the Chair position to be posted, Susan didn't put her name in. She was content to remain a full professor with more time to engage in research and prepare for her classes, even though her graduate classes took her away from her family three nights a week.

Scenario Two: A Faculty Member Who Yearned for the Bigger Image and Salary of an Administrator

Robert always held himself in high esteem as a scholar and researcher—this despite the majority of faculty in his department knew he rarely published or presented at conferences. But Robert was highly polished and dressed as though he had just exited a *GQ* magazine cover shoot. At committee meetings across campus he would sit in a strategic position, open an expensive leather portfolio, and wield a Mont Blanc pen, before sharing the latest joke. And the campus higher-ups were duly impressed—as were new assistant professors. When the inexperienced Chair was due to be evaluated, Robert shared a few of his thoughts with the new assistant professors. They joined with a couple of associate professors and went to the Dean saying their current Chair's performance was inadequate and that Robert would be a good leader to move the department forward. The Dean removed the Chair and named Robert the permanent Chair, to the delight of the newly hired assistant professors. However, the full professors and most of the associate professors were dismayed by this.

As time went on, Robert didn't manage to get the day to day department work accomplished. He made demands of some faculty members that were unprofessional. The Dean mentioned the problems to the University President who was looking for someone to serve in a cabinet position. He thought Robert would be perfect for the job and promoted him across campus to a much higher paying position. Many senior faculty in the department were relieved to have gotten rid of Robert, as he had been a minimal contributor as a colleague and not very successful in his role as Chair. The new Department Chair was fair and got things completed in a reasonable amount of time.

Robert was now responsible for writing reports for the university for the state. But leopards generally don't change their spots. Robert didn't get the reports finished on time, and they didn't appropriately represent the university—often lacking important details. One essential report had to be rewritten—twice. Finally the President had to rewrite the entire report himself.

Robert was then given a golden parachute to leave the university. All five of the new assistant professors as well as the two associate professors who had supported Robert's move to chair the department left for other institutions. Robert retired to Florida to play golf with a much larger pension than had he stayed as a faculty member.

Scenario Three: Lack of Leadership Skills

Herman wanted to be Department Chair despite lacking good organizational skills, always getting things done late and being a stickler for perfection in work done by others. It was a relatively modest-size department with a collegial faculty. Finally, the Dean appointed Herman to serve a three-year term as Chair. While the department had been moving along fairly steadily with few bumps under the previous Chair, Herman was determined to make it a well-oiled machine. He changed the job descriptions and responsibilities of the secretaries and support staff even though their union contracts spelled out their duties. Herman switched faculty members' schedules and class times and, in a couple of cases, reassigned faculty to teach new preparations. When Thanksgiving break arrived, Herman had a complete meltdown and ended up in the hospital. A month later he was still unable to perform his duties. An Acting Chair was named, and Herman never returned to be Department Chair.

6

Moving into Retirement

When it comes to retirement, it is likely that the professor or administrator will ask, "Where has the time gone?"

Increasingly faculty are delaying retirement due to changes, for example in public universities' pension benefits. The uncertainty of knowing if a pension will be cut has caused many faculty to stay an additional year or more, putting aside additional funds for their golden years. Some institutions are cutting or reducing other benefits, such as health insurance for retirees. And then there are a number of faculty who elect never to retire until they have health concerns or their level of attentiveness declines, as they love teaching, conducting their scholarly research, and serving on committees with colleagues.

Some faculty count with joy the days until the actual day of retirement, looking forward to shedding the stress of a full-time job. Some retirees teach as part-time faculty at a university or community college, work in another career that offers much less stress, or volunteer in their church or community. Other reasons for retiring include caring for an ill spouse or aging parent, the need to help in raising grandchildren, personal health issues, and an inability to keep up with technology changes.

Other faculty choose to extend their teaching and research for another year or two—even going so far as to submitting a letter of retirement with a date and year specified. Others, who should retire because they start to falter in their ability to handle the stress and the workload, stay too long. The decision to retire can stem from a "feeling" or the "reality" of not being able to stay on top of academic responsibilities. In the case of the latter, the faculty member has perhaps overstayed his/her time in the position with students being the recipients of less than sterling instruction in the faculty member's classes.

It is not uncommon for faculty to find it very difficult to leave the academic world of which they were so much a part of for twenty to thirty-five years or longer. How do you give up something easily and joyfully that has been so much a part of your life, something that you have poured your heart and soul into when times were easy and when they were difficult? How do you wake up one morning and adjust to not going to work? How do you go to sleep at a reasonable hour at night because you don't have to prepare for class and grade papers?

Many times, prior to or after retiring, they leave in a huff and distance themselves from colleagues in their department or college. Emails go unanswered, Facebook pages disappear, they move out of state without telling their colleagues, or they just ignore any communication attempts and end up fading away. Why could this be? Here are some possibilities:

- The faculty member feels that withdrawing from his/her relationships with colleagues will lessen the emotional toll of his/her life's changes.
- The faculty member feels that the department is just tolerating him/her and counting the days until he/she retires. This is more or less a lame duck phenomenon; that is, "You are here but you won't be here long enough to make a difference in this department."
- Perhaps the person has been asked one time too many: "How much longer until you retire?" Or "Why are you still working?" The faculty member may interpret these questions to mean he/she is no longer wanted in the department or college.
- It is possible that his/her expertise of twenty to thirty or more years has gone unappreciated—and this hurts.
- The faculty member is no longer asked to be on committees in the department or across the university—and this hurts.
- It is possible that it is just too painful to be reminded of his/her own vibrant, younger self, and retirement is just too emotional.

You may hear a soon-to-retire person say he/she does not want a reception or send–off party. The colleagues left behind are usually baffled and think back to make sure they have not offended the retiree. The whole departure just becomes awkward.

On the other hand, some people know how to retire gracefully. They announce their retirement, follow through on the date, accept a send-off party, and listen to what people have to say about their illustrative career. Yes, there could be a few tears or a slight choked up feeling, but they are able to get through it with a smile and a thank you. That is the best way to approach retirement.

You may find that retiring requires some counseling to find out why it hurts so much, but it is important not to take the "hurt" out on the people around you. It is not their fault that your career is coming to an end. Remember that you are also a role model for people who will retire after you do. Hopefully you will muster up enough emotional energy to walk away on a positive note. You don't want to be remembered as the negative and grumpy person who got mad because you got older.

Preparing for Retirement

Just as a faculty member prepares for tenure and promotion, so too should he/she give thought to the eventuality of retirement. At least two years prior to your estimated retirement date, visit with your university's Human Resource (HR) person in charge of retirement. This individual is bound by law to maintain confidentiality, so unless you mention your intentions to a colleague or administrator, no one will know your plan to retire. The HR person can estimate what your retirement pension will be. If you teach at a public university you can go online and see what the pension estimate is by plugging in your present salary, estimated raises, and number of years you intend to teach before you officially retire. You can do likewise to determine an estimate for your Social Security benefits. Keep in mind that if you live in a Windfall Elimination Provision (WEP) state, as mentioned earlier, you will receive reduced Social Security benefits even if you have the necessary forty quarters. If you are married and have forty quarters toward Social Security benefits, your spouse will receive reduced benefits under the Government Pension Offset (GPO).

You need to create a mock budget (see below), anticipating your first two years of retirement. Consider all expenses. Do you need a new vehicle? If so, you may want to purchase one prior to retiring and pay for it before you retire. Or perhaps you'll receive a lump sum benefit payout for unused sick leave or vacation time that you could put toward a new vehicle. If you are planning to do a substantial amount of traveling via driving your own vehicle after you retire, a new or newer vehicle may be an essential purchase.

Example Monthly Budget Plan for Retirement

Monthly Pension from University		$_____
Social Security		_____
Investment Income (Stocks/Bonds)		_____
Annuity		_____
	Total Monthly Income	$_____
Expenses		
Housing		_____
Utilities		_____
Heath Ins./Medicine		_____
Vehicle and Maintenance		_____
Food		_____
Entertainment		_____
Travel		_____
Hobbies		_____
Misc.		_____
Savings		_____
Investments		_____
	Total Expenses	$_____

Will you have expenses with supporting or caring for a parent or parents? Children in college? Older children who have returned home? Grandchildren who may live with you or need assistance with college or other school costs?

Health care for yourself, spouse, or significant other needs to be part of your consideration. Are you eligible for Medicare? Will you fall under the Affordable Care Act provision, or will your university benefits include health insurance at a reduced rate?

Do you have long-term health care insurance? Obtaining such insurance prior to retiring as part of your college's insurance plan will usually be much less expensive than getting it on your own. Women in particular are more likely to need long-term health insurance care,

Campus of the University of British Columbia, Vancouver.

as women tend to live longer than men. Having a rider that increases your long-term health insurance daily benefits will increase your annual premiums but is worthwhile in the long run as the cost of nursing home care continues to rise.

Typically new retirees tend to travel far more during their first two years of retirement than they did while working full time. International travel can be expensive, particularly if the value of the U.S. dollar is not high in comparison to foreign currencies. Setting aside a pool of funds in advance of your retirement to use for travel during those initial two years of retirement is a wise idea. Some faculty buy tax-free municipal bonds in amounts of $5,000, staggering their due date years to have ample funds to cover their retirement travel in the coming years. Others purchase CDs whose maturity dates are staggered to come due each year to provide travel monies. Typically purchasing tax-free municipal bonds and staggering their due dates has been a better financial investment than doing likewise with CDs.

Will you stay in your current home during retirement or downsize or move to a new location? Since retirement is a major change, remaining in your current home for at least a year may provide you with a greater feeling of security—particularly if you have family and friends nearby. Also, by the time you retire, your present home may be paid for, so you won't have a mortgage to worry about each month. Or will your current house need upgrading—will you need to replace appliances, update the bathroom to be more "senior" accessible with hand rails and a shower instead of a soaking tub, paint the interior or exterior of the house, or replace the windows or roof? Ideally these changes should be done prior to your retirement.

If you elect to downsize, it will take time to get rid of unwanted items, furniture, books, and the like. Some people find that they prefer to sell their larger home and purchase a smaller one in the same area while also purchasing a small house in a warmer climate (or cooler climate depending on where your university is located). State income tax, sales tax, and local property tax rates are all considerations when thinking of a second home.

If you would like to explore other locales in other states, planning vacations during your winter and spring breaks to places that pique your interest may be a good way to determine a retirement locale. When you finally select a place, renting a condo or house for a year until you determine the exact location in the area you want to live is advisable. Margaret and Harry had vacationed in Arizona for several years and, once they retired, left Boston to escape to their newly purchased home in Tucson. But after two years, they realized they weren't keen on living full-time in Arizona and put their house in the desert up for sale. Ruth's husband passed away just prior to her retirement but she forged ahead and purchased a house in the mountains of Colorado that she and her husband had dreamed of for years. Although most of her family lived in St. Louis, Ruth loved the solitude of her new home and seeing the grandeur of the Rocky Mountains out her windows. Max and Marcia had both taught at a University in Texas and when they retired, they bought a dream home in New Mexico. After six years in retirement, Max developed dementia and they sold their house and moved into an apartment in Madison, Wisconsin, a few blocks from their son.

When looking at new locations to live, don't forget to consider locations near universities, as they tend to offer links to the arts, concerts, and even continuing education courses just for seniors. Some even have retirement communities such as The Village at Penn State. Some universities have adjunct positions that need to be filled. Ron retired and moved from Minneapolis to Tucson where he teaches patent law.

For the more venturesome faculty, retiring to a foreign country may be attractive. Spain offers relatively inexpensive living as does Costa Rica. The Caribbean has numerous island retreats that some retirees find appealing.

Some retirees want to volunteer in their community with such organizations as Meals on Wheels, the local food pantry, Habitat for Humanity, literacy centers, during or after school programs, park district sports programs, hospitals, animal rescue centers, and other organizations. Certainly there are a wide variety of needs to be filled. Signing up for two years with the Peace Corps is yet another alternative that appeals to some retired faculty as a way to share their expertise with people in other countries.

Perhaps you would like to stay put and ease into retirement by teaching fewer courses over one or two academic years. Some universities permit faculty to retire with the understanding that they can teach one or two courses a semester or continue to conduct research funded by grants while retired. Such arrangements should be made in writing so everyone is clear on the expectations and duration of the agreement.

Roles of Administrators and Colleagues

How can administrators and colleagues support faculty as they enter the final years before retirement? Here are some things administrators and colleagues should and should not do:

Do:

- Go to them for their impressions of pre-retirement, telling them you would like to learn from their experience.
- Include them in outside activities in which colleagues participate, e.g., going out to dinner, to a movie, to conference presentations.
- Respect them and the ideas they offer in faculty meetings. Yes, they may say something you do not agree with but be professional in responding.

- Rather than say, "When are you retiring?" it would be better to say, "You sure will be missed around here when you decide to retire." After hearing a statement like that, it is likely they will tell you on their own when they are planning to retire.
- Allow them to teach summer courses, if requested. Larger classes or hectic schedules should not be given to faculty who are on their way out.
- Recognize their contributions at the institution and include them in any written publications at the university.
- Nominate them for awards across the university that you believe they deserve.

Don't:

- Pressure them to retire. This is a federal offense.
- Ignore their ability and desire to participate in important decisions and projects if they are showing an interest.
- Minimize their accomplishments by saying, "Oh that was a long time ago. That was then and this is now."
- Say it is better to have younger professors on a Search Committee because they will identify more with the candidates. Remember, it is pretty impressive for a candidate to know that faculty like the university well enough to stay their entire career.
- Neglect to offer a send-off reception.

If a faculty member's upcoming retirement is handled well, the person can positively end his/her career and most likely remain in touch with colleagues after leaving the department.

The Retirement Decision Is Up to the Faculty Member

One thing to remember is that the way you retire is totally up to you. You are the person in control. No one at the university should have the power to make it a negative experience.

After the party, you go home, but you still can be connected to the university. So you may want to ask the Chair of the Department, the Dean of the College, or the President of the University if they can still use your services in a limited capacity after you retire. In some states you are able to draw your state-funded public pension and you can still work at the university as long as you don't pass the set amount of money you are allowed to earn while drawing your pension. If the university doesn't need your services, you'll need to pursue a job or activity that will make you happy. It is clearly difficult to work so hard for so many years and then come to a screeching halt. As nice as it may sound to wake up the first morning after retirement and have no academic work to do, it is something that needs some getting used to. Be patient with yourself and with people who may be giving you too much feedback about your life and what you need to do to be happy. Recognize this time as an adjustment period.

After the adjustment period, people will often say, "I can't believe I didn't do this sooner. Retirement is wonderful. I guess I didn't realize how much stress I was under as I worked through to full retirement until it was over and so was the stress. I don't have to go to a conference to travel. I can travel where I want to and enjoy relaxation."

The key word to retirement is "graceful." Hold yourself together and do not become bitter. It takes too much emotional energy to harbor negative feelings. Think of your career from the following positive perspectives:

- You chose a career in which you stayed and felt productive until retirement. That does not happen for everyone.
- You had to have been a productive faculty member because if you weren't you would not have received promotion and tenure.
- You have published and conducted research, and thus you have made a mark in your field. You have earned a name for yourself.
- You have acted as role model for younger faculty over the years. You have guided graduate assistants. Toward the end of your career you were looked at as a person who had experience and expertise in many areas.
- You will be remembered by your students for many, many years. It is not unlikely that you will hear from students long after they have left your classroom, they learned so much from you. Some will hunt you done via the Internet, university email, Facebook, Twitter, Instagram, and whatever new technology that comes along.
- You have credentials and you can move on in your life by making presentations or writing journal articles and books or serving as an adjunct teaching at a four-year or two-year school in an area of the country desirable to you.

As you look backward and forward in your life, hopefully reminiscing about both will make you smile. You did it—you should feel great! You entered the Ivory Tower with some uneasiness because you didn't know completely what was expected of you and now you are walking through the same door as you leave. Hopefully your head is held high.

EPILOGUE

Scenario One: Failure of Administration to Be Sensitive to Senior Faculty's Contributions

George had been a faculty member for thirty years in the department. Well respected across campus, he was also a superb recruiter of graduate students for the doctoral program. In recent years, George typically presented at a national conference every couple of years, but he hadn't published anything in the last five years. George was moving toward his retirement, although he never talked about it. The department hired a new young Chair who began calling faculty into his office. When it was George's turn, the Chair expressed concern over his lack of scholarly productivity. George pointed to his nearly all-white head of hair and said, "How do you think these got here? I'm not getting any younger."

One of George's great joys was chairing Doctoral Dissertation Committees. While he served as a Dissertation Committee Chair, he carefully orchestrated the selection of the other committee members for their expertise in research and specialized aspects of the field; he wanted members who would be ideally suited to supervising doctoral candidates in conducting research and producing quality dissertations. The new Department Chair informed George that he could no longer serve as sole Chair of Dissertation Committees but would have to have a Co-Chair who had a strong, active research agenda.

While two other senior faculty colleagues merely shrugged the same information off, George felt he had been blindsided. He was deeply hurt and felt that his contributions over the year were not being recognized by this young Chair. Although he possessed the skills to be a productive researcher, George had always preferred to hobnob with the current University President and Provost as well as his own Dean at various campus meetings as well as devote a large amount of time in luring students

113

to the program. Rather than gear up with a research agenda, George made an appointment with HR Department and submitted his retirement letter to the Dean.

The lack of tact by the new Chair resulted in a significant turnover, as five senior faculty retired within three years or took other positions within the university. The number of doctoral students dropped as well. Moreover, since George was single with no living relatives, he had originally planned to leave a generous donation to the college. Due to the circumstances that caused him much ill will, George wrote the university out of his will and put in the local community hospital instead.

Scenario Two: Announcing Retirement Intentions Too Soon

Susan had had a wonderful career in academia, having taught thirty-two years. Her college offered an incentive of a paid semester-long sabbatical to senior faculty if they submitted their letter of retirement two years early. Susan confided to a friend at another university that she would never do that. When her friend asked why not, as the college offer of an entire semester off with pay seemed very generous, Susan's response was surprising. Susan said, "I might as well be dead. As soon as everyone knows I'm retiring, no one will listen to me or inquire as to my take on an issue or proposed change."

Unfortunately at most institutions, once an individual announces his/her plans to retire or leave, colleagues and administrators intentionally or unintentionally fail to engage that individual in discussions of events impacting the department. Perhaps it is human nature, but individuals such as Susan, who helped build a strong department and who have been very productive scholars, feel abandoned and put aside. For Susan to announce her retirement and then be ignored, as she had observed happen to other aging faculty, would spawn a general feeling of worthlessness—and she would have no part of it. Instead of speaking openly about her retirement plans, she went to the HR office two months prior to her retirement date, submitted her letter of retirement, and told no one about it until the last department meeting of the year when she requested to move for adjournment since "this will be the my last faculty meeting ever."

Scenario Three: Respecting Newly Retired Faculty

Jill was retiring as Chris became Chair. He didn't take the time to get to know Jill. Jill didn't have any close relatives—the university had been her life. She lived modestly even though she was one of the highest paid faculty members on campus. Jill took great pride in supporting university events such as the symphony and art exhibits. Over the years she had made it a point to take new faculty to lunch and inform them of local events. Her intentions had been to leave her estate to the university and her church. However, once she retired, no one from the university contacted her. She changed her will and left her entire estate to her church.

Scenario Four: Working with Senior Faculty as They Adjust for Retirement

Bill was an old-timer at his institution. He had seen it all. He'd mentored a young colleague over the years who ended up as the college's Dean—and who no longer had the time of day for Bill. But the Department Chair understood the need for supporting senior faculty. Carol, as a young faculty member at another institution, had watched while senior faculty were seemingly cast aside and made to feel worthless. She was determined that would not happen on her watch. She made certain that each semester she would have lunch or breakfast with each senior faculty member, just as she did with each new faculty member. She believed she could glean information that would be useful—oftentimes learning the history of issues that went back to years prior to her own arrival on campus. Carol also was adept at matching senior faculty as mentors for new faculty. Carol believed that a Department Chair needs to have a sense of what is taking place throughout the department, and frequent interactions with all of her faculty were essential if she was to stay on top of things.

Carol liked Bill's bluntness; he presented issues clearly and concisely and was always fair and objective—something she very much valued. When Bill told Carol he thought he wanted to retire, Carol asked him how she could assist. Bill was a strong instructor and well liked by students despite his bluntness. He wanted to teach a course a semester for the next three years. "Done!" Carol announced. Bill retired on his terms, feeling he had made a difference and was still a valued part of the university.

References

Coe, A. 2013. Being married helps professors get ahead, but only if they are male. *The Atlantic.* http://m.theatlantic.com/sexes/archive/2013/01/being-married-help-professors-get-ahead-but-only-if-theyre-male/267289/ (Retrieved January 19, 2013).

Farris, P. J., and Werderich, D. E. 2011. *Language arts: Process, product, and assessment in diverse classrooms*, 5th ed. Long Grove, IL: Waveland Press.

National Education Association. 2014. Social Security Offsets: Frequently Asked Questions. http://www.nea.org/home/16819.htm. (Retrieved January 17, 2014).

U.S. Census Bureau. 2012. *Statistical Abstract of the United States: 2012*. Washington DC: Author.

Index

119